Restructuring Your World

Becoming a **REAL** Christian in the real World

Young Adult Edition

A Guide to Making God Your Counselor

Dr. Brenda J. Robinson
and Brooke Cason

XULON PRESS

Restructuring Your World — Young Adult Edition
by Dr. Brenda J. Robinson and Brooke Cason

Printed in the United States of America

ISBN 978-1-60647-135-7

www.newdesire.org

www.xulonpress.com

What Young Adults Are Saying About the Author and Her Writings

I have been involved in Christian music ministry all of my life and I have never met anyone like Brenda Robinson.

Some call her Dr. Robinson; to me she is just Brenda. From the moment we met, we knew our friendship was a divine connection and she has become an invaluable spiritual mentor to me as well as a trusted friend. I know that she prays for me every day.

I've had the privilege of working with New Desire in the recording studio and Brenda always begins our sessions with a devotional and prayer. One morning during the devotional she, her daughter-in-law, Brooke, and I began discussing some of our own struggles in our lives and began sharing prayer requests. At one point I absently commented, "Hey, why don't you write a book for *single* women? We could use the help!" By no means am I taking credit for the inspiration of this book; rather, I am thankful that Brenda is using her God-given gifts to minister to a group of people that desperately needs Godly counsel and encouragement.

She would never consider herself to be anything special, but whether she's teaching, writing, singing, or cooking her fabulous homemade biscuits, the love of God in her heart is evident to everyone she meets.

I am proud to call her my friend.

Lauren Talley, 25
The Talley Trio, Morristown, Tennessee

Each day we come into contact with hundreds, if not thousands of different people. Whether it is in a classroom, on the job, or on the street, we meet some people we will never see again, and some who will make a lasting impact on our lives. When I was twelve years old, I met one of those people who would change my entire outlook on life.

Brenda Robinson is an established singer, songwriter, and author. She has a story unlike anyone I have ever known. It is a story of pain, heartache, perseverance, and joy. It is a story that will change your life as well, if you will let it.

Some people, like footprints in the sand, will wash away with time, but others will influence you in ways you could never comprehend. Brenda Robinson, more than anyone, has inspired me to be the best that I can be in everything that I do. My mentor, my hero, my friend – I could only hope to have the kind of faith of a person like Brenda, who met adversity head on and never gave up.

Jessica Guinn, 17
Crossville, AL

Brenda Robinson has been a major inspiration to me. I have been saved since I was 8 years old but I never really had a personal relationship with Christ. I first heard Dr. Robinson speak a little over 3 years ago at one of her Women's Conferences. My life hasn't been the same since! It was at this Conference that I realized that I hadn't been living my life as I should. I wanted to know more about having a daily walk with Jesus Christ. Studying her books and listening to her speak has put a burning fire in my life to have a personal relationship with Him. As teenagers we are all faced with peer pressure. Dr. Robinson has taught me that studying the Word and staying grounded in your faith will help you resist the temptation to give into peer pressure. When I face trials and difficult decisions in my life, I just run to the Word of God. No matter what the situation is, I always find peace in knowing that he's by my side all the way. Brenda, I just want to thank you for the example that you live and teach.

Brooke Cason has also had a big impact on my life. She just shines with the love of Jesus. Thank you for always being there for me. I love both of you dearly.

Lauren Parten, 16
Royston, Georgia

Brenda Robinson is a faithful and genuine person. As I have set under her teachings and read her books I stand amazed at what God has done in her and through her. She has a relationship with Jesus Christ that is so real you can see it through the loving yet truthful words she speaks. But, what I find even more amazing is that she lives and functions in her day to day life 100% what she teaches. I had the honor and privilege to travel with Dr. Robinson and New Desire as a fill-in soprano recently and witnessed first hand their personal lives. I am proud to say that everything Dr. Robinson says, as well as everything she does is God centered and bathed in prayer. Who and what you see on stage, as well as on television, is exactly who and what she is in private. She knows that God is her all and all and she lives in that truth. In her book "Made Over" she shares that God's desire for us is to have an abundant, joyous life. However, we must put all of our faith in Him as we allow Him to renew and rejuvenate us from the inside out. Her books and conferences have taught and encouraged me, by example, how to have a relationship with Christ that is lasting and life changing!

Michelle Nalley, 22
Calhoun, Georgia

Table of Contents

Acknowledgements

This book is dedicated to all young ladies who are willing to stand strong in their walk with the Lord and who refuse to compromise their convictions to be accepted by their peers.

To Brooke, my precious daughter-in-love, I thank you for all the hard work you have put into co-writing this book with me. It is always a joy to work with you. New Desire Christian Ministries is blessed to have you as not only a singer, but now a writer. I love you with my whole heart.

A special thanks goes to Angie Gentry for all her hard work and labor in seeing both the adult and young adult editions of this book completed. Angie, I love you and I thank you for taking loads of responsibility off of me. You are a blessing from the Lord.

It is with great passion and desire that I live for the Lord. It is with an even greater passion that I serve Him for the sake of others. This book is written for every person who needs to know that God loves them. It is written for those who are searching for relief in the midst of their trials, and victory in the heat of the battle.

My prayer is that every reader will read with an open heart and mind so that God can give you the same passions and desires I have. I love you all. May God bless all who seek Him.

How Do I Know This Book is for Me?

*M*ost young adults live their lives in complete denial about *their* life issues and how well they deal with or handle them. For most, they do not *deal* with them; instead, they usually *dwell* in them to the point that they succumb to peer pressure often resulting in wrong decisions. The pressure then becomes too heavy to bear and they find themselves searching for love, significance, and acceptance in all the wrong places. Their flesh overtakes them and satan embraces their weaknesses. Their self esteem deteriorates and they begin to doubt God and themselves, as well as those closest to them. When left untreated, the end results are devastating and destructive. I challenge you to keep reading to see if this book is for you.

Perhaps you are in search of significance, acceptance, love, or perhaps you just long to love yourself but cannot seem to get there. Maybe you find yourself with no motivation or desire. Could you be experiencing rejection, frustrations, and doubts about things and people in your life where you once felt secure? Are you battling the realms of burnout, mental instability, emotional distress, and spiritual defeat from an overactive lifestyle? Do you feel a void inside in spite of all of your extra curricular activities? Does it seem that everyone around you wears on your last nerve and you just want to be alone?

Perhaps you find yourself to be in abusive relationships, not only physically abusive but mentally and emotionally as well. Do you find yourself feeling like there is no way out of these relationships or that you cannot do any better for yourself? Maybe the threats of those you are so close to has put you in a state of fear to the point you feel paralyzed from ever being free and your life being different than what it is now.

How many times have you cried out to God, your peers, or even your parents in desperation because you felt abandoned and hopeless? Have you found yourself at times blaming God or your loved ones for your condition? Does church or God motivate you, or do they cause you to experience feelings of guilt or bondage? Do you attend church because you have a longing to be there to worship and serve, or do you attend church to satisfy and impress others and your parents?

Are you one of those who think you can handle anything life dishes out all on your own? Are you a Miss/Mr. fix it? Do you think talking with others and sharing your problems is completely out of the norm for you and to do so would be a breach of your privacy? Are you worried that if you did share your burdens that you would be ridiculed by your peers?

Are you a person who is one personality in public but someone totally different at home and around those closest to you? Do you constantly worry about what others are thinking or saying about you? Does paranoia and insecurities control the types of relationships you build?

Could it just be that life has been so hard on you that you are afraid to trust others, especially God whom you have not seen? Are you haunted by your past and feel you cannot escape it? Are you carrying such great hurt that you will not allow God or anyone else into your life? Are you a person of anger and rebellion? Maybe you are just stagnant and you feel nothing for God or anyone else?

If you have answered yes to any one of these questions, then this book is especially for you. If you are ready for a change, this book will help you. The key to sanity and victory is *discipline* to study and learn. If you are serious about a relationship with God, you will experience a beautiful transformation in every area of your life. It all begins with prayer, prioritizing, and perseverance. You can do it!!!!!! Spend time with God. He is the key to changing your world. Make God your counselor and your mentor.

Introduction

*I*t has been through many years of spiritual mentoring, lay counseling, and just being a listener that has prompted the publishing of this study guide. I have gleaned great knowledge from listening to and praying with those whom God has sent my way - knowledge of the pain and turmoil that people face internally that others may never know they carry. I have listened to the fears, the tragedies, and the haunting past that still controls the lives of many young people today. I have prayed with them, cried with them, hurt with them, and even asked God to let me carry their pain for them.

Galatians 6:2 says, *"Bear ye one another's burdens, and so fulfil the law of Christ."* Through the years, I have tried to fulfill this Scripture only to have failed miserably. My heart was to fix them and to help release them from the pain. I realized all of my efforts were not working. With much prayer and seeking God on this matter, I came to realize I did not have the power to mend broken hearts. However, I could point them to the One who transformed me when I was in their shoes. God began to reveal to me a system that would change and free all who would use this method with determination and sincerity. I was the first one God used this system on. Over twenty years ago, I was freed, changed, and spiritually ignited. God created this just for me and it worked. My life as a child of God, and all the other roles I carry, has never been the same. He has laid on my heart to share this with you. The Bible teaches us to seek Godly counsel and to confess our sins, weaknesses, hindrances, and even our past to others we know we can confide in. **Proverbs 11:14** says, *"Where no counsel is, the people fall: but in the multitude of counsellors there is safety."* The Bible also teaches that God is the Great Counselor, the One to whom we must go to above all others. **Proverbs 9:6** says, *"For unto us a child is born, unto us a son is given: and the government shall be upon his shoulder: and his name shall be called Wonderful, Counsellor, the Mighty God, the Everlasting Father, the Prince of Peace."*

As more and more young adults came to me for spiritual guidance, I began using this system on them. For those who wanted change and a closer walk with God, the study guide was very effective and freeing. For those who wanted to pacify their parents, peers, teachers, etc., the system did not work for them. It was only a temporary fix for their pre-existing and present problems.

This study guide is not error proof or the quick fix. It is simply a tool to guide you to the presence and power of God - your Wonderful Counselor. If this study is used with determination to overcome through Christ Jesus, your world will be forever changed. You will come to know God in a way you never thought you could, and you will live for Him with purpose and desire. Regardless of your age, God's Word and His presence in your life can fill the void that you are looking to the world to fill. In Christ and in Christ alone is where you will find significance, love, and acceptance.

The key to any study tool is to complete what you start and to apply to your life what you learn. 2 **Timothy 2:15** says, *"Study to show thyself approved unto God, a workman that needeth not to be ashamed, rightly dividing the word of truth."* This study will help you to have a more intimate relationship with God. It will reveal to you the things you need to deal with that have become stumbling blocks in your life. It will force you to examine yourself and to deal with your past and your present circumstances. As these things are dealt with, you will find yourself living in and for Christ. You will find freedom from the past, joy for today, and hope for tomorrow. May God bless you as you restructure your world according to God's plan.

Chapter One

Young Shattered Lives

A Story from My Past
by Brooke Cason

Do you ever feel rejected? Do you ever feel alone? Do you ever feel abandoned? Do you ever feel like you can't do anything right or good enough to be pleasing to others? Do you feel that no matter how good you are it's not good enough? Do you ever feel suicidal?

Let me introduce you to my best friend. Of course, I can't call this person by name so I will be referring to them as FRIEND. Friend was a very popular person all the way from kindergarten through high school. Friend was always on the honor roll, was top in the class, was everybody's friend, and didn't have an enemy. This person was what I would call a role model. I was very close to this person and knew everything there was to know about them...I thought. Friend was voted most popular, best looking, wittiest...this person had it all going for them. Friend had a picture perfect family. Friend's siblings were all very close. Their parents were very involved in all that we did. They came to every sport event and every school function. On the surface, Friend seemed to have it all.

I can remember being teenagers and fighting the battles of hormones, peer pressure, and trying to fit in to a certain degree. We both had wonderful families who went to church and brought us up in the ways of the Lord, but we were still common day teens. We wanted to be in the midst of all that was going on with all of our other friends. We wanted to attend the parties, ride the town, hang out together, etc. All of those things that teens wanted to do, so did we. We were no different than the rest of the gang.

Friend's world seemed to be perfect on the surface, but inside there was so much hurt, anger, rebellion, depression, etc. Friend's world was about to shatter. I can remember like it was yesterday. We were playing our rival team in football. In our hometown, like most everywhere, high school football is major. We had been celebrating for the game all week long to pump our football team up. We didn't have a good football team at all, and we didn't believe in our hearts that we would win the game, but for the team's sake we pumped them up. The cheerleading squad had made a Bulldog out of papier-mâché to burn the night before the game was to be played. The whole town showed up for the pep-rally that night. It was an exciting night. Of course game day was the next day. Did we get anything accomplished at school that day? NO! We were all too excited about the big game. We had another pep-rally for the school on game day. All of us cheerleaders reported to the gym and got ready. Before entering the gym, my friend looked at me and told me, "Make this the best yet because it will be my last one." I hugged Friend and said "Rest assured it will be the best yet just for you!" In my mind I didn't think anything out of the ordinary. I thought that Friend might have an orthodontist appointment set for the date of our next pep-rally which would be the last one for the season. Keep in mind that Friend had never drank alcohol, had never done drugs, or had sex before. A picture perfect teen...on the surface.

The game was unbelievable. The score was 7-0 at half-time with us being 0. We never thought that the game would only be 7-0. We figured that we would be plastered on the score board by half-time. In the second half of the game, we came back and tied the game in the last minute 12-12. Can you imagine how excited we all were? We kicked for the field goal and "IT WAS GOOD!" At this time everybody ran out on the field. I noticed that when Friend came to hug me, Friend was drunk. I couldn't believe what I was seeing. Friend was hanging out with the wrong crew at the ballgame. They provided Friend with alcohol. This was the first time Friend had ever had a drop to drink. Of course it didn't take much. Friend looked at me and said, "Let's go celebrate with the rest of the team and all of our friends." I told Friend that I didn't want to go, but Friend insisted on going. I went to be with Friend and watch after all the others. I was so afraid that Friend was going to go overboard. I was right. I looked up after I arrived at the party, and Friend was vomiting profusely. I kept holding Friend until they felt better. I called Friend's brother and told him that a few of us sober ones would bring Friend and his vehicle home and for him to be waiting for us. I didn't want Friend's parents to know what was going on because I knew this was out of the ordinary. This was the first time Friend had ever drank. Of course, Friend was busted by their parents. They threatened to send Friend to a re-hab that following Monday after school. Friend was not an alcoholic, but was accused of being one.

We were all standing together waiting on Friend to arrive to school on Monday morning to aggravate Friend about the weekend. Friend's parents were very strict, but they went to extreme sometimes. Friend was not an alcoholic, just a teenager. Am I saying that what he did was right? NO! It was wrong, but Friend didn't deserve to have to go to re-habilitation for a one night thing. Needless to say, Friend never showed up for school. At 8:15 a.m., one of our other friends said that he wanted to go call and check on Friend. The bell rang for homeroom and we never got to call. After school, I had cheerleading practice. I can remember being in practice and one of our friends entering the room with tears in his eyes. He walked straight over to me and embraced me in tears. I kept asking,

"What is wrong?" He finally told me that our friend had committed suicide. I'll never forget that moment, how I felt, or what I said. I couldn't understand why God had allowed this to happen.

As a teen losing my best friend, I had a lot of unanswered questions. I wanted someone to blame. I tried to blame Friend's parents, myself for not understanding what was going on, and our other friends for not recognizing the cry for help. You never know what someone is facing on the inside. Friend felt like a failure constantly. Friend had everything going for them. Friend was and honor roll student, top of the class, had a lot of friends, full college scholarships, and a wonderful family...what more could you ask for? I had to realize that no one was to blame but my friend. Friend made the final decision. Friend's world was not at all what I thought that it was. It was not a happy world. It was a world full of depression, disappointment, anger, hatred, and so much more.

You see, Friend didn't only hurt the family that was left behind. Friend left a lot of friends hurting as well. The day Friend died, a part of me died as well. There has been a void in my life every since the day Friend committed suicide. Life will never be the same for any of us who remember Friend. Friend was so full of life and joy on the outside, but on the inside Friend was slowly dying.

What I want you to learn from my friend is that you do not have to hide who you really are. You cannot fight the battle by yourself. Let others know when you are hurting. You are surrounded by people who love you. Do not live in a fake world. Face the facts and deal with them. Do not accept the voice of satan when he tries to tell you that you are nothing but a disappointment to your parents or other family members. Satan wants you to feel unloved, insecure, depressed, etc. Reconstruct your world with God in control. Make God the center of your circle. Ask Him to construct your world according to His will for your life. Get rid of all the negatives and live for the positives. Remember that life will deal you a box of rocks. It is your choice to either make them stepping stones or stumbling blocks. Do not feel like you have to live a perfect life to be accepted by your family and friends. We are human and we will make mistakes. God will pick you up and wipe off all your sins. Your parents will pick you up, hold you, and let you know how loved you are.

I would like to challenge you to study this book with an open heart and mind. Please receive what God has in store for you. Our goal is to mentor you while you discover who you really are in Christ. Allow God to fix the wrongs and make them right. He is the Father of chastening. Allow Him to correct you and direct you into a path of righteousness. The Almighty God has allowed me to see when my world is looking destructive, and He loves me enough to show me how to correct my priorities.

Please know that I love you and have prayed for each one of you that receive this book. My prayer is that you will learn how to live a life in Christ, to be a peculiar people, and to overcome peer pressure and the need for material possessions. Pray for God to open your eyes to who you really are deep down inside. Do not let satan fool you while reading this book. Pray that God will allow you to accept a change in your life.

A Story From My Past
by Brenda Robinson

Unlike Brooke, whose life was filled with popularity, acceptance, and honor, my life was completely opposite. As a young adult, I was not raised in a Christian home. Rather, I lived in a home of great dysfunction – an alcoholic father, a very sick mother, eight siblings, and great rejection, ridicule, and criticism from my peers. I did not have the perfect role model in a father. I could not go home to his arms of love. Instead I went home to his hands of abuse. There were many times I felt like I was being a parent to my parents. My story goes like this...

I could hear the licks being passed as I lay in my bed. At midnight, I was still awake listening to my mom cry as my dad beat her in his drunken stupor. I was twelve years old and terrified that my mom would not live through the night. I remember mom always telling us to stay in the bed if dad ever came home drunk. She always told us to pray for her and that God would protect her from his beatings. That night I prayed and cried until I cried myself to sleep. The next morning mom woke me up for school all bruised and battered, but she gave God the glory for another beautiful day of life.

My whole childhood was lived in abuse, dysfunction, peer pressure, poverty, rejection and low self-esteem. There were not very many happy childhood days for me. At home, there was fear, at school there was criticism and rejection. I never knew when my daddy was going to go into one of his rages and start beating on mom or one of my siblings. There were nine of us children, so he had plenty to choose from. Mom would always step in and take our place. Dad only hurt us when he was drinking. She would step between us and tell us to run.

At school, it was a different type of abuse. There was the abuse of criticism and rejection because I did not live in a nice home. I lived in a 20' x 30' block house with no indoor plumbing. It was very noticeable when the school bus stopped to pick us up and let us off. All the children would point their fingers at our house and laugh, especially when they saw the outdoor bathroom behind the house. They criticized my clothes, my shoes, and my hair. They told me I was ugly and unaccepted in their clicks. They said I would never be anything in society because of my poverty and my alcoholic father. The other students would talk about me, laugh at me, tell lies on me and make me the laughing stock of the classroom. In the bathroom, they would shove me around; on the bleachers, they would push me down. The only thing that kept me sane in school was the fact I enjoyed learning. I enjoyed my teachers and the challenge of achieving. I was an honor student in every grade. I focused on my studies and making my mom proud of me. She had enough going on in her life without having to worry about my grades.

It's very hard to fit into society when you have nothing to offer. The social pressures begin in about kindergarten these days and swell to enormous levels by fourth and fifth grade. By the time you hit sixth, seventh and eighth grades you are already swallowed up in five things – the battles of:

- Acceptance
- Popularity
- Fashion
- Socialism, and the
- Power of influence

We often pattern our lives for adulthood based on the way we were treated as young people. We long to be accepted in our adolescent years by those around us, not only those we go to school with, but even our parents, teachers and other adult figures in our lives that we love and respect. In all actuality, the adolescent years are considered to be from the age of twelve to twenty years old. These are the years when you are the most influential, vulnerable and rebellious. These are the years when you will make wrong decisions based on the influence of others because you want to be accepted and popular by the "in" crowd.

When I was twelve years old, my life was forced into maturity level much deeper than most twelve year old girls. I was working a public job and helping my mom pay bills while going to school. My peers ridiculed me because I would leave school and walk two miles to my job so that I could help make ends meet. They all went home to their families and enjoyed what most people considered a normal life. They were able to participate in after school sports, other activities, spend time with friends and do homework at home. I did my homework on my break at work or after I got home from my after-school job which was often 10:00 or 11:00 p.m.

I didn't have time to deal with the acceptance, social, popularity, fashion and other issues that teens and singles have to face today. The issues were there, I just chose not to be controlled by things that wouldn't hold any future value in my life. I admit at times it would have been nice to feel as if I was a part of the crowd or at least acknowledged by my classmates, but due to my poverty level and my lack of fashion statements, I was pretty much ignored or criticized.

By the time I reached junior high school, I was known as the drunken man's daughter and the smartest girl in the class. Everyone else would try to steal study notes from me. The other students would try to cheat during tests by sitting close to my desk so they could copy my paper. I fixed them though. I would cover my answers with my hand or I would sit in a desk straight in front of the teacher's desk. I figured if they couldn't acknowledge me as a person, I wasn't about to let them use my knowledge to help them pass a test. I guess by being the ninth child, I was a little mischievous in a few things myself. I learned a lot just by watching my older siblings.

In the seventh grade, I accomplished several things. I won several gymnastics awards. I was chosen to model for the Sears Spring and Summer Wear Catalogue. I won the spelling bee for our grade. All of these things would be coming to fruition at the end of the year. I was so excited that mom was so proud of me. I felt as though I was finding myself, my place in society and my place in the world. The other students began to respect me and some even befriended me. My world was looking up, and every day after school, I walked to my job with a spring in my step and a smile on my face. I couldn't wait to get home every night to tell mom about my day at school. She was always the greatest encourager of all nine of us children.

One particular day after school, I got a call on my job to walk to the hospital because my mom had been taken there with a heart attack. My job was only two blocks from the hospital, so I ran as fast as I could to meet the rest of my siblings there. Mom was in ICU. They told us that she was critical, that she had actually had two heart attacks, and her heart was severely damaged. At twelve years old, neither my mind nor my heart could fathom life without my momma. She had always taught us children the importance of being saved and having a relationship with Jesus our Savior. She had taught us the power of prayer and the promises of God's Word. I started praying for God to heal my momma's heart and to make her well and bring her home. We were all a very close family. She had taught us the importance of sticking together and loving each other even when it seemed our worlds were falling apart. This was a time that we had to do that. God heard our prayers, healed her heart and brought momma home. The doctors said she wouldn't be able to hold a job after that, so we pulled extra hours to make ends meet. We never could depend on daddy financially. He was always in and out like the wind. He spent his money on wine, women and gambling. I can never remember him even buying me a pair of shoes. I loved him though. He was still my daddy.

Mom's health declined more and more during my seventh grade year of school. She had another heart attack and two back surgeries that caused paralysis to the point she couldn't get out of bed without help. This is where my world began to crumble. I couldn't stand the thoughts of going to school and leaving my mom home alone. My other siblings were married with families and jobs. I felt a deep responsibility to take care of my mother. I would leave for school every morning crying because I knew she couldn't even get up for a drink of water. My whole day at school was filled with worry and fear for my mom. My older brother and I were the only two children still in school and living at home. There were days I would sneak away from school and walk home just to see about momma. The school would call and I would get into trouble, but in my heart, getting into trouble meant nothing when it came to taking care of my momma.

Before the end of my seventh grade year, the doctors had determined that mother could no longer be left unattended, so I was taken out of school about mid-year to stay home with her. I lost the opportunity to model for the Sears Catalogue, to represent our grade for the spelling bee, and I wasn't able to go to state for gymnastics. Again, my heart wasn't focused on those things. I knew my responsibility was to be there for my mom. From the time I was twelve until I was sixteen years old, I helped care for her along with my other siblings.

Before being taken out of school by permission of the authorities, I did suffer from some peer pressure. The other students reminded me daily how poor our family was and how unattractive I was. They would tell me daily I was ugly. They would tell me I was a misfit for society and there would never be a place for my family and me in the social realm. They said my family and I were failures and an embarrassment to society.

These are words very hard for a twelve year old girl to hear. I wanted to show them what I could become. My mother had taught me that I could be anything I wanted to be. I could achieve anything I set my mind to. She even taught me that in life there are never failures; only lessons if we make our mistakes stepping stones instead of stumbling blocks. She taught us that we could do all things through Christ Jesus, but without Him, we could do nothing. I look back on all my years of mistakes and stepping-stones, and I realize my mother knew exactly what she was talking about.

Young people, this is what I have to teach you through the writing of this book. My heart is to get you focused on the right things, Godly things, things that hold future and value. My prayer is to structure your world at a young age that consists of godliness, righteousness and moral standards that set examples of holiness. You must start now building yourself a foundation of truth, respect and boundaries. You must purpose in your heart to be an influence in the lives of others rather than be pressured by others' influence on you.

I want to be your spiritual and moral mentor. I can be that to you through this book. I can help you with tough decisions. I can point you to Scriptures that will give you God's mind on your behavior, choice of friends and lifestyle.

God can help you overcome any obstacle you will face in life. He will help when you are struggling with temptation and peer pressure. He will be your way of escape when the enemy seeks to devour you, and He will cradle you in His arms when you are hurting. God loves His children and I love you too.

I do not want your teen years to be lived out like mine were. I believed everything the other kids said about me. I lived my life feeling rejected, like a failure, and totally ineffective as a human being. All of these feelings were based on what others thought and said about me - others who really didn't matter; people I would never see again or would see very little after school.

I always received positive influence and words of encouragement from my family. Momma taught us that one word of negativity could destroy a thousand words of positivity. She was so right. For every word of encouragement and hope I was getting from my loved ones, I was allowing the negative words of my peers to destroy the words of those who loved and believed in me. Those negative people are gone from my life now. All they left behind were bad memories and scars of how cruel people can be and how deeply words can cut. My family who loved and encouraged me are still here. They are still believing in me and supporting me. My world revolves by the power of God and the love of Jesus Christ.

Friends, if you are allowing your world to operate and revolve based on the influence and opinions of your peers, you could very easily be deceived just as I was. You, too, could become the victim of negativity and cruelty. Is it possible that you are already caught up in what others are saying and doing? Are you listening to the lies of your peers over the love of your family and encouragers? I challenge you to reread carefully Brooke's insert of her high school experience. Then, challenge yourself to complete this study. Find a friend to do this study with; a friend who will keep you honest and accountable. I would recommend your Mom or Dad or even a sibling. Any of those would be a perfect partner to study with. Purpose in your heart to be your own person with your own set of values. Make sure God is the center of those values. You will be able to overcome any obstacles the world and the devil throws your way. You will also be able to achieve anything in life you purpose in your heart to accomplish.

I love you, God loves you and I will be praying for you. Remember, you are never too young to change your world for the glory of God and for your good.

It only takes one small mistake to lead you into a lifestyle of sin and deception. When satan gets a hold on your mind, he will fill it with things that make your flesh feel powerful, independent, and successful. He will convince you that you do not need God. When this happens, it is just a matter of time before wrong decisions, negative influence, and satanic forces lead your world. They will look and feel good to the flesh, but they will lead to destruction.

There are many areas of our lives that are controlled by our feelings and emotions. School, sports, and college are areas where we are dominated and manipulated by our minds rather than by true facts and what our heart knows is the right thing to do. Places of pleasure often control how we live our life because as the Word of God teaches us, we become "lovers of pleasures more than lovers of God." Therefore, we get addicted to the pleasures that take away the reality of what is really going on in our life. We make our pleasures our god. We put them before God and even before those we love. You see, the reason our world appears shattered is that our mind is filled with wrong things. We operate our life under false feelings, temporary fixes, and worldly influences. We live trying to reach the world's standard of living when God is calling us to be a peculiar people.

Why is depression rampant in our country? Why is the suicide rate higher than it has ever been? Why are there more addictions to sex, drugs, alcohol, credit cards, and food in this country than any other country? It is because we are operating our life under our own power with our own thinking rather than operating under the instructions of God's Word, God's power, and God's mind.

We take our every weakness and find something in the world to make it go away. We allow our feelings to override facts. There is a song we sing that says, "You don't have to believe the way you feel." The reason our lives get in the poor condition they do is because we do believe our feelings. Have you ever studied the word "feelings" in the dictionary? The noun definition is the act or condition of one that feels; an emotion. Happy, sorrow, fear, and anger are feelings. These words are what we build our lives on. Most of the time, this is how it goes for people. If a person is full of happiness, they go out and live it up. They spread true happiness with everyone until they have spent out. Happiness is a temporary feeling. However, in Christ Jesus it can be replaced with an everlasting gift of joy that is also a fruit of the Spirit. Joy, peace, and love are also feelings. They are positive feelings that are from God. These are the feelings that we should build relationships on. Joy is always inside you. You may not always feel joyous, but you can always call on God and He can produce joy within you. In the hardest of times, you can have joy as a resource for your life. Joy is not just based on feelings; it is based on a relationship with God. Sorrow or grief is another fleshly feeling. It controls our moods and our behavior just like happy does. When we lose a loved one to death or divorce, we react to the feelings of sorrow and grief. Some people go into a deep depression; some withdraw or get angry and bitter. All of these are responses to what they feel.

Negative feelings, such as sorrow, fear, and anger produce stress, anxiety, and depression, and they cause our world to tilt. These feelings can be overcome with the help of God. Positive feelings that come from God cause our world to balance out. Do not misunderstand me. Negative feelings are real and painful and they are deep within us. They are a part of our being, but we must not allow them to operate our lives, control our behavior, and drive our personalities. We must not allow negativity to override what God can do for us.

Our feelings are just that – they are feelings and we must deal with them. If we dwell in them, then we live and operate in them. We then build our lives around them, and we end up with negative results, such as the following:

Wrong Choices	Paranoia	Over-Confident
Negative Influence	Insecurities	Loneliness
Addictions	Peer Pressure	Withdrawal
Worldliness	Rejection	Depression
Worry	Denial	Deception

As we try to navigate our way around and through this stressful maze we call life, we find ourselves exhausted, overwhelmed, burned out, and hopeless.

Like the examples in the beginning of this chapter who lived young shattered lives, our lives are in no better shape. We may not be as deeply entangled yet, but if we do not get a grip on our feelings and emotions, we will be victimized by the flesh, the world, and satan. A church sign read, "Dear Lord, I have a problem-it's me." This is such a true statement. So many times we blame our problems on everything and everyone but ourselves. Until we can face the fact that we must define our inner problems and realize they are *our* problems and not everyone else's, then our world will never be balanced.

I challenge you to make a list of your priorities and the things that are controlling you. Discover who you are based on your thoughts, feelings, and behavior.

After you have made your list, re-evaluate your life based on what is inside. Begin making changes that will restructure your world to one that will fill your mind, heart, and entire life with a desire for God and righteousness. If your life is already there, then keep it structured by re-examining your life on a daily basis.

On the following page, you will find a testimony of someone who, after a mis-structured world, learned that only God can bless your life and honor your standards of righteousness.

Personal Testimonial
Shared by permission.
Names have been changed to protect identity.

*First and foremost, I want to thank my Lord and Savior Jesus Christ for bringing me up out of a horrible pit, out of the miry clay called my past. I thank God for giving me the opportunity to share with you my life as a teenager. Please understand that I am not proud of the life I lived as a teen, and much prayer was put into the decision to share this testimony. For many years, I have lived in shame and regret, wishing every day that I could go back to my teenage years and make some major changes. However, my past is gone and can never be changed. My only hope is that through this testimony, you will realize that decisions you make as a teen will follow you for the **rest of your life**. My prayer is that you will see that you do not have to give in to peer pressure and be like everyone else. You **can** live for God and make a positive difference in the lives of your peers.*

My Life as a Teen

My teenage life started out like any other. In school, I was an A & B student. I was in the band, sports, chorus, drama club, and Beta Club. I was a good student, never getting into trouble, and I was liked by all my teachers. I was very shy and only had a few people that I really considered friends.

At home, my parents were still married and they loved both my sibling and me. My parents made sure that we attended church every time the doors were open. They had pretty strict rules that they expected to be followed. They chose the music that I was allowed to listen to and they tried to choose my friends, or at least they discouraged hanging out with certain people. We occasionally had a family Bible study, and we didn't discuss things such as sex, drugs, or alcohol. Those topics were "taboo" in our home. I was very determined to please my parents, and often my decisions were based on what was expected of me instead of what I wanted for myself.

When I was almost 16, the youth group of my church went to a youth retreat. On Saturday night, I went through an emotional experience during the service, that consisted of tears and walking the isle during the invitation. Afterwards, my mom asked me, "So what did you do tonight, sis?" I replied, "I got saved", even though I did not pray, confess my sins, or surrender my life to Christ. I knew that's what she wanted to hear, so that's what I said. From that moment on, I tried to live the Christian life. I kept going to church and was baptized. I was a good person. I didn't curse, drink, have sex, or do drugs. My friends were mostly other members of the youth group of my church.

Soon after the youth retreat, the church had some issues arise and many people left. We began visiting other churches. My family went from attending church every time there was an opportunity, to attending church only for Sunday morning worship. It was painful for me to leave the church where my friends were, and in the hurt I decided that "if this is what the Christian life is all about I don't want it, and I certainly don't need it."

I had grown tired of my parents dictating what kind of music I could listen to, what friends I could hang out with (they didn't want me hanging out with friends whose parents were divorced), and what I could or could not do, so I decided I would live life **_MY_** way. I became very rebellious, and my attitude became one of "I do not care"!

My first venture in my new life of doing things my way was attending a concert in Atlanta with a couple of friends. My parents knew I was going – what they didn't know was what I was taking with me. I had purchased a 12-pack of beer to carry along so that I would be sure to "really have a good time". I had never had a drink of alcohol, so I was drunk before I finished half of them. The friends that I was with could not believe that *I* was drinking. That was so out of character for me. And what was even more unbelievable was that I was not that quiet, shy person I had always been. That night I had come out of my shell!

I loved my new life of rebellion. I went out every weekend with friends, and somehow I would end up drunk. Since my parents were very strict and not very understanding, I could not call them. When it was time for me to go home, I would get in my car and drive myself home (usually a 20-30 minute drive). Because I wasn't that "good girl" anymore, I began to make new friends that also liked to party. All of the friends I had been hanging out with (the ones from my church youth group) didn't hang out with me much anymore.

My attitude was one of just not caring. I did not care what anyone thought of me. My thoughts became consumed by what kind of partying I would do during the upcoming weekend, and school became an afterthought. Soon, my grades began to fall. I received my first C on my report card and my parents were so highly upset. I'll never forget the conversation my mom and I had. She told me, "If you don't straighten up and quit wasting your life, you will never be anything. You will never amount to anything if you don't get your act together!" That really made me angry, but I began to believe it. I became even more rebellious, and even more uncaring! Why should I care? I would never be anything, right?

Soon, I was out of the Beta Club because of my grades. I was still partying every weekend and still driving my drunken self home. For the most part, my weekends consisted of hanging out with friends. Occasionally, I would go out on a date, but I never had a real serious relationship… until I met Bob.

Bob was 5 years older than me and already in college. He was tall and slender with blonde hair and blue eyes – a true heartthrob. We went out on dates for a couple weeks, and I just totally fell head over heels in love with him. We decided to take our relationship to the next level. One night, instead of him picking me up, we just met in town. I had already been drinking when we met, and we decided to go somewhere quiet. We talked, and kissed, and talked some more. Then, one thing led to another, and we had sex. From that point on, we would just meet up and go off… to have sex. One night, I told my parents I was spending the night with a friend. This was a friend that was older and owned her own house. So I went out with this friend, got drunk, and then I met up with Bob. Bob and I went back to my friend's house and had a night filled with smoking, drinking, and sex. I thought it was just wonderful waking up beside him the next morning, even if I did have a massive hangover. Bob went back to his apartment and I got ready and went to meet my family at another church we were visiting. I guess going to church the next day made me feel better about all the sin the night before. In reality, I had such a hangover that I didn't want to be in church and I certainly didn't get anything out of the service.

Bob and I "dated" for about a year. I truly thought I loved him. After all, I had lost my virginity to this guy. I was very much *emotionally* attached to him. He was everything to me and I had given him everything. And then one night after we had been "out", he lowered the bomb. He wanted us to see other people for a while, or at least for the summer. He was going home for the summer, and I guess he didn't want to have to be faithful to someone he wouldn't see for several months.

I was absolutely devastated. I felt like my heart had been totally ripped out of my chest. Somehow, I knew that we probably wouldn't be seeing each other when he came back to school the next fall. He was ending it for good.

Since I had an "I don't care" attitude, I acted like it was no big deal. No one knew just how bad my heart had been broken or how bad I was hurting inside because of the thought of not being with him.

After Bob and I quit seeing each other and he went home for the summer, I didn't date for a while. I would just hang out with friends – smoking, drinking, and just having a good time.

I started dating a guy that was 15 years older than me. Of course my parents totally disapproved of me seeing him, which made me see him even more. We only dated for a few weeks and then we both moved on.

After I quit seeing the "old man" I met another guy that was closer to my age but was not from my community. Instead of trying to give him directions to my house, I offered to meet him in town. We went out and tried to get to know each other. He showed me a picture of a small child that he said was his son. I thought surely he was kidding, so I pushed that information to the back of my mind. Our first date was fun and uneventful. When we got back to town, he walked me to my car and kissed me goodnight.

We went on a couple of other dates that were uneventful as well. We had fun getting to know each other. On our fourth date, I met him in town again. After we went out, he wanted to go somewhere quiet. I soon found out that he knew his way around the town better than he had let on. After driving for a while out of town, we ended up down a dirt road. He showed me a knife and a gun in the car which really scared me. He began to kiss me and touch me all over. I asked him to stop and he said, "You know you want me". I told him I had no intention of having sex with him and asked him again to stop. He then became somewhat violent and kissed me even harder than ever. He started trying to undress me and I was fighting him all the way. He was a lot stronger than I was and he held my arms by the wrist with one hand while he kept trying to undress me with the other. He put the knife up to my neck and scraped me with it enough for me to bleed a little. He let me know right then that I would do whatever he wanted me to do or I would be sorry.

I really thought he was going to kill me and fear overtook me. All I could think about was that He would leave me dead off on a dirt road and no one, not even my friends, would know who I was with or where to start looking for me. I was crying and begging him to take me back to my car, and I fought him with all my might. He was becoming even more agitated and violent with every minute. By this time, I was pretty well undressed as was he. He was on top of me holding me down. He would grab my throat or my hair to show his agitation, he hit me a few times, and he didn't hesitate to remind me of the knife and gun. Without going into too many details, he forced himself upon me. I was so scared that he was going to kill me that I finally quit fighting and gave in to his demands. I was forced to do things that night that I never wanted to do. He just kept saying, "You know you want it".

I didn't go home that night – I stayed with a friend. I didn't share the details of the evening with her, but she knew when I couldn't quit crying that something was wrong. She saw the "scratch" on my neck and the multiple bruises on my body the next day. I never shared the details of that night with anyone, out of fear-fear of what he would do to me if I reported him to authorities. He called several times over the next week, but I never took the calls. For several weekends he showed up in town. I was sure he was following me, so I made sure I was never alone and that my car was never left in town unattended – I didn't know what he might do. He finally quit coming to town and I never talked to or heard from him again.

From that point on, I decided to never have another serious relationship with a guy. I would never let some guy hurt me the way the others had. I hung out with friends until all my friends started dating guys. Then, to avoid being by myself, I began going out with 2 or 3 different guys every weekend. I was building quite a reputation as someone who was "easy". Everyone thought that if I was dating that many guys, surely I was having sex with all of them. That was not the case, although I was not opposed to going off and making out with them.

During my senior year in high school, I went to another concert with friends. I was drunk before I got there and the place was filled with smoke – everyone there had been smoking pot. Between the alcohol and the pot smoke, I was totally wasted. I found myself leaning on my best friend's boyfriend. I was on one arm while she was on the other. His hands were all over me but I was too intoxicated to care. Afterwards, he and I met up to "finish what was started at the concert", and then I went to spend the night with that best friend.

By the spring of my senior year in high school, I was well on my way to becoming an alcoholic, and my grades reflected it. I was not just drinking beer or wine coolers on the weekends anymore; I was drinking beer, mixed drinks, or some kind of liquor almost daily. I even got drunk one day before school. I thought that was pretty cool, until my teachers began to suspect that I was either intoxicated or high on drugs. Fortunately, they didn't call my parents!

Just before I was to graduate, a girl and I had problems. She began to call me names and taunt me after school one day. Since I was such a "bad" girl, I convinced her to go to a park in town (you know, I wanted us off of school property) so we could get our issues settled – once and for all. Several people ended up at the park with us, and of course she and I didn't just talk things out – we got into a fight. I broke her nose and beat her up pretty good. When I saw her in school the next Monday, she was black and blue all over. Her eyes were black and her face and lips were swollen. I looked at her, and then I just laughed in her face.

I finally made it to graduation. Of course, there was the graduation party afterwards where I, along with my friends, celebrated the accomplishment. Bob showed up to congratulate me, but we just talked awhile and then we parted ways… for good. The next week, some friends and I headed off on our senior trip. The first night was not too eventful – just basically getting settled in. The second night, however, was a different story. A friend and I ended up having approximately 18 shots of tequila, while another friend had sex with numerous guys – one guy at a time with everyone else watching. I couldn't believe that she was doing that but I was too drunk to stop her and she apparently was too intoxicated (and possibly high on drugs) to care. By the time my friend and I got back to the condo, we were both vomiting profusely, and that continued throughout the night. I was sick for several days after that one night of partying. I was glad to go home at the end of the week.

I entered college in the fall after my high school graduation and the partying just intensified. I can remember being taken home by a guy I was dating and vomiting outside while he held my hair out of my face. Needless to say, I didn't date him long.

My grades were nothing to brag about during my first semester of college but I did pass. I kept partying anytime I had the chance… until I started dating a guy that had been a known alcoholic. Surprisingly, the night we met, he was drinking a soda (with no alcohol added) and shared with me that he had accepted Christ as his Savior and that he was not the same as he had been. We started seeing each other, but he would not tolerate me drinking around him and he wanted me to go to church with him.

We didn't date a real long time, but he is the one who got me back into church. I began going regularly and my parents and I found a church that we liked so we joined it. I got very involved in everything about the church – from the youth group, to the choir, to attending Sunday school every week. I was trying to get my life together. I quit drinking and partying and soon found that any spare time I had was consumed with activities at church. Once again, I was trying to live right and I wasn't "sinning" as I had been, but there was still a void.

That void was that I was trying to live the Christian life without Christ. God began dealing with me and I realized that I was lost and on my way to hell. I realized that trying to live the Christian life without Christ was just an **IAN** (**I Am Nothing**) life. I accepted Christ as Savior and have been forever changed. It is amazing what He has done and is doing in and through my life. The Bible says in **2 Corinthians 5:17,** *"If any man be in Christ, he is a new creature: old things are passed away; behold, all things are become new."* I am a living testimony of this verse. I am not the same person that I was during my teenage years. No, I am a new person in Christ.

However, my actions as a teen have followed me for many years. Every time I see one of the girls that I called a best friend in high school, I am reminded of all the things we have done together. She'll say "remember when we did" this or that, and then she'll say, "Those were the good ole days. We had a lot of good times then." I don't see her often enough for her to witness my new life in Christ. In all honesty, those were not "good times". There is no goodness or fun in vomiting profusely or waking up the next morning in a fog and with a splitting headache because of alcohol intoxication. There is nothing but shame in waking up beside a man, who is not your husband, but rather just someone you have had repeated sex with. There is no glory in vulgar language or in having sex with guys because you were too intoxicated to realize or to care what you were doing, or just because you want to be accepted and you think that sex is what it takes to fit in.

I am still known as a fighter with some of the guys who witnessed the fight that I was in. They don't know how much I regret that I fought with the girl and that I laughed in her face afterwards. I often wish that I could turn back time and just walk away from her. The Bible teaches in **Luke 6:27-29**, *"But I say unto you which hear, Love your enemies, do good to them which hate you, Bless them that curse you, and pray for them which despitefully use you. And unto him that smiteth thee on the one cheek offer also the other; and him that taketh away thy cloke forbid not to take thy coat also."*

I realize now that driving while heavily intoxicated with alcohol was very selfish and, just to put it plainly, stupid. Fortunately for me, I was able to get home without injuring or killing myself or someone else. I realize now that it was only by God's grace and protection in my time of ignorance. Some people are not so fortunate. One of my friends that never drank and always lived a Christian life suffered the loss of her sister – she was killed in a vehicle accident. The driver of the other car was driving under the influence of alcohol. Many innocent people are killed everyday because others make the decision to drive while intoxicated.

Alcohol and drugs affect your perception and your ability to make sound, logical decisions. The effects of those substances alter judgment. I made many decisions under the influence of alcohol that I normally would never have made otherwise. Driving home while intoxicated was one of them. The largest regret I have is making the decision (while heavily intoxicated) to have sex and continuing to have sexual relations throughout my teenage years with different guys.

Young ladies, you do not have to have sex to feel loved or accepted. If you are really loved by the person you are dating, he will not even suggest it. Sex for men is a physical need. For women, sex is emotional. The decision to have premarital sex has followed me since the first time I made it. The entire time I was in sexual relationships, I was constantly worried about becoming pregnant or contracting a sexually transmitted disease. Several years after Bob and I stopped seeing each other, I ran into his best friend in town. He gave me the shocking news that Bob had cancer and was receiving treatments. He didn't know what kind of cancer he had (which I thought odd since the two of them were so close), he just knew he had cancer. I was terrified. The first thing that ran through my mind was, "What if he really has AIDS, and they are just calling it cancer to keep everyone from knowing the truth?" I lived in that fear for years!

If you are in an abusive relationship, get out of it! You deserve so much better and you are worth so much more. There is someone who will love you without being physically and emotionally abusive. Do not be afraid to terminate the relationship. There are people who love you and will protect you from the abuse. Report the abuse to the proper authorities. You might save your life and the life of a future victim.

This world is filled with societal pressures that you will face every day. The only way to overcome those pressures and to fill the void in your life that you are looking to the world to fill is to have a personal, intimate relationship with Jesus Christ. There is no peace or hope in the world. You will not find it in sex, drugs, alcohol, or relationships. You will not find it by making the best grades, being the best on your cheerleading squad, your ball team, or in the band. It can only be found in a relationship with Jesus Christ. He alone can give you the *"...peace of God which passeth all understanding..."* **(Philippians 4:7)**.

The relationship with Him must be a *personal* one. It cannot be based on your parents' bank account, your parents' societal position, the kind of home you live in, the clothes you wear, or the car that you drive. It cannot be based on how often you attend church just because your parents make you or how good you are. You must accept Christ for **yourself** and let Him transform you into a new creature in Him. Then you will no longer worry about what your peers think of you. You will begin living in Him and they will know that you are a "peculiar people".

You can be a positive influence on your peers and they will remember you as the person that lived for Christ regardless of what others thought of you or tried to get you to do. But how do you take a stand for God when everyone around you is urging you to partake in sinful pleasures?

First of all, *"ye must be born again"* **(John 3:7)**. You must accept Christ as your Savior. You must realize that God loves you and wants to save you. You may have already been living a life of sin and think that God cannot love you because of your actions. **Romans 8:35-39** says, *"Who shall separate us from the love of Christ? Shall tribulation, or distress, or persecution, or famine, or nakedness, or peril, or sword? As it is written, For thy sake we are killed all the day long; we are accounted as sheep for the slaughter. Nay, in all these things we are more than conquerors through him that loved us. For I am persuaded, that neither death, nor life, nor angels, nor principalities, nor powers, nor things present, nor things to come, nor height, nor depth, nor any other creature, shall be able to separate us from the love of God which is in Christ Jesus our Lord."* Your sin, no matter how big or little you think it is, cannot separate you from the love of God. He does not love your sin, but He does love you, the sinner.

Salvation is not difficult. You must *admit* that you are a sinner and realize the penalty of sin. **Romans 3:23** says that *"...all have sinned and come short of the glory of God"*. **Romans 6:23** tells us that the penalty of sin is death. *"For the wages of sin is death; but the gift of God is eternal life through Jesus Christ our Lord."* You must *believe* that Jesus died to save you from sin and arose the third day victorious over death, hell, and the grave. **John 3:16** says, *"For God so loved the world that he gave his only begotten Son, that whosoever believeth in him should not perish, but have everlasting life."* **Romans 5:8** tells us, *"But God commendeth his love toward us, in that, while we were yet sinners, Christ died for us."* You must be willing to *confess* your sins. The Bible says in **1 John 1:9**, *"If* *we confess our sins, he is faithful and just to forgive us our sins, and to cleanse us from all unrighteousness."* Finally, confess Jesus as the Son of God and your Savior. **Romans 10:9-10** tells us *"That if thou shalt confess with thy mouth the Lord Jesus, and shalt believe in thine heart that God hath raised him from the dead, thou shalt be saved. For with the heart man believeth unto righteousness; and with the mouth confession is made unto salvation."*

Second, *"pray without ceasing"* **(1 Thessalonians 5:17)**. Your school may not allow you to pray out loud. Praying does not have to be done with your eyes closed or in an audible voice. You can pray in the middle of class, in the midst of being pressured by your friends, or at any other time that you need strength from God. If you are saved, you are His child. He will hear your prayer if it is prayed from the heart. He will give you the strength to stand strong in Him. **Isaiah 26:3-4** says, *"Thou wilt keep him in perfect peace, whose mind is stayed on thee: because he trusteth in thee. ⁴Trust ye in the LORD for ever: for in the LORD JEHOVAH is everlasting strength."*

Third, study the Word of God and hide His Word in your heart. **Psalm 119:11** says, *"Thy word have I hid in mine heart, that I might not sin against thee."* If you study God's Word and hide the Scripture in your heart, the Holy Spirit will bring it to remembrance when you need to witness to someone or when you need strength to stand against the pressures you are facing.

I know that it is difficult being a young adult in this world. I understand how you feel when it seems that you are all alone and you have no one who cares or who you can confide in. Just remember, you are not alone. Find someone to talk to that will pray for you and give you Godly, Biblical counsel instead of opinion. If you do not feel that you can talk with your parents about the issues and pressures you are facing, find a mentor that you can confide in.

I love each of you and I pray that you will not make decisions that will result in you living in regret as I have for so many years. I would give anything to turn back time and change my life as a teenager, but I can't. My teenage life haunted me for years. Only last year did I cry out in desperation to God and asked Him to get me passed my past. He was faithful to release me from my past and He has given me the courage to share this testimony with you.

Make a decision today to live for Jesus despite what others think of you. You are special to God and His thoughts of you are all that matters!

Learning How to Choose Mr. or Mrs. Right

When you reach the age that your parents allow you to begin dating, what do you look for? Are you looking for someone who is popular and good-looking, or are you looking for someone who is sincere and Godly?

You should be looking for someone who shares the same or similar beliefs in God that you do, someone who will respect you and receive you for who you are. There are so many young adult relationships that are entangled with dysfunctions. It is important that the companion you choose to date or to eventually consider your boyfriend/girlfriend is God-fearing, drug and alcohol free, respects their own parents, respects themselves, and especially you.

In the world we live in today, it is not a bad idea to check their backgrounds. For example, question their friends and those they hang out with. Get to know their family. **Know who you are with!!!!** Just because these people may be faithful church members does not mean you are safe when you are alone with them. Herein lies your responsibility. If you are keeping yourself right with God and pure from the world, God will let you know the wolves in sheep clothing. You must establish standards of what you want in a companion, and you are the only one that can set those standards. Make them high and Godly standards.

The Lord has already appointed His companion for you. Your responsibility is to keep yourself holy and untainted from the world so that when His time arrives to join you with your companion, there will be no regrets. You should look for someone who has the love of God in them, who has future goals, and who wants a career and a family raised in the Word of God.

I have heard so many horror stories from young adults, male and female, who found themselves in abusive relationships while just dating. It is vitally important to free yourself of such relationships. It is never too late to remove yourself from life threatening situations. Never allow fear of someone to prevent you from going to your authorities. Once they are exposed of their abusive behavior, you are not only free of them but you may also be saving the life of their next victim. Never let the enemy tell you that you have to settle for less than the best. The best is God's chosen one for you. **Isaiah 40:31** says, *"But they that wait upon the LORD shall renew their strength; they shall mount up with wings as eagles; they shall run, and not be weary; and they shall walk, and not faint."*

Setting Yourself a Standard

Joshua 24:15-16 *"...but as for me and my house, we will serve the LORD. [16]And the people answered and said, God forbid that we should forsake the LORD, to serve other gods."*

Below is a guide that will help you to righteously choose not only your friends, but intimate companions – those who you may choose to have intimate relationships with. I challenge you to tear out this page and put it in a place so you have to read daily, or if not daily, weekly. If you feel that your standard has been compromised, this guide will help you to get back on track.

1. God must dominate your entire life – thoughts, actions, and decisions.

2. Never allow your peers dominate you.

3. Be your own person. Do not change for anyone.

4. Keep your body sexually pure until you are married.

5. Stay away from those who criticize, persecute, and reject you.

6. Never compromise your beliefs and convictions to be accepted.

7. Let your companion know up front what your standards are and that you do not compromise for anyone.

8. Do not be influenced by drugs, sex, and alcohol.

9. Ask your companion if they are willing to attend church with you.

10. Make sure your companion believes in God.

11. Make sure you are always a Godly example in front of your companion.

12. Never stay with or settle for someone abusive.

13. There should always be a curfew time.

14. Get to know those who are connected with the one you are contemplating a relationship with.

15. Question the integrity, future goals, and family values of your companion.

Teen Connection
by Brooke Cason

Love Your Enemies

Luke 6:27-35 *"But I say unto you which hear, Love your enemies, do good unto them which hate you, [28]Bless them that curse you, and pray for them which despitefully use you. [29]And unto him that smiteth thee on the one cheek offer also the other; and him that taketh away thy cloke forbid not to take thy coat also. [30]Give to every man that asketh of thee; and of him that taketh away thy goods ask them not again. [31]And as ye would that me should do to you, do ye also to them likewise. [32]For if ye love them which love you, what thank have ye? for sinners also love those that love them. [33]And if ye do good to them which do good to you, what thank have ye? for sinners also do even the same. [34]And if ye lend to them of whom ye hope to receive, what thank have ye? for sinners also lent to sinners, to receive as much again. [35]But love ye your enemies, and do good, and lend, hoping for nothing again; and your reward shall be great, and ye shall be the children of the Highest: for he is kind unto the unthankful and to the evil."*

Many times we come into contact with people who are very rude and cast judgment. They make fun of us because we do not wear the up-to-date name brand clothing they wear, drive the fancy cars they drive, or hang with the crowd they run with. I have learned that being different is not so bad. It is very pleasing to God. The Bible says in **Luke 6:27-28** *"But I say unto you which hear, Love your enemies, do good unto them which hate you, [28]Bless them that curse you, and pray for them which despitefully use you."* Your peers that don't like you and make fun of you are what you would consider to be your enemies. The ones who use and abuse you and only want something to do with you when they need something are also what I would consider to be an enemy. God commands us to love these people and to do good to them. We should pray for them and show them the love of God in our daily walk.

As you read Dr. Robinson's life story as a child, you saw that she was made fun of constantly. The kids made fun of her home, the clothes that she wore, and the way she looked. None of this is anything that she could help. Her mother worked three and four jobs to make ends meet. She was doing all that she could do to provide for her family. You never know what someone is living in and having to deal with at home. Most of the time the parents are doing all they can do and the kids cannot control their raising and economic status. If you are the one being mocked, do not let it get to you. There is an old saying, "kindness kills the cat." If you are the one doing the mocking, stop and think about what you are saying and how bad it is going to hurt the one that you are talking about. They cannot help where they come from. You do not want to be the reason someone has low self-esteem.

In **verse 35** it says, *"⁵But love ye your enemies, and do good, and lend, hoping for nothing again; and your reward shall be great, and ye shall be the children of the Highest: for he is kind unto the unthankful and to the evil."* It is our duty to be good to others and hope for nothing in return. We should always be kind and not expect anything in return. If you see someone needing some love and affection, give it to them by being kind to them and showing them that God loves them and cares about them. If you see someone that needs guidance, give them the Word of God. Lead them to Him! God commands us to be kind and helpful, not rude and judgmental.

In this day in time, we find ourselves being caught up in what everybody else is doing. We don't have to join the crowd and be like everybody else. Be kind and loving. When someone is causing you grief, show them God's unconditional love by loving them anyway in spite of what they are saying about you. If you are the one causing the grief, stop and think about what you are saying and what kind of long-term effects your harsh words are going to have on the one you are making fun of. Do not be the reason this person contemplates suicide. Think Godly in everything you do and say.

Do you experience mockery from others? _____

Do you love your enemies? _____

Are you the one that is making fun of your peers causing them grief? _____

_____

Are you the reason that others have low self-esteem? _____

Do you want to be more Christ-like and loving to others? _____

List some ways that you can show God's love and compassion to those you have

seen in need? _____

_____

_____

_____

_____

De-stressing Your Life

Below is a system that will help you restructure your life on a daily basis. Follow this system when you feel you are overwhelmed, stressed, and need to feel the presence of God in your life.

Define the stress and record it below. _____

_____

_____

Explain how it makes you feel inside. _____

_____

_____

Describe how you respond to the stress. For example, do you feel anger, fear, nervous, anxious, etc? _____

_____

_____

Who or what provoked you? _____

_____

_____

You have just dealt with and confronted your stress and its issues by answering the above questions. Now, let's free ourselves, clear our minds, and give it all to God with the following steps:

- Focus on God and His goodness by listing one issue of praise to God for today.
- Take a moment and thank Him for the day and the fact that He helped you through it.
- Acknowledge Him as your Ultimate Guide, Helper, and Comforter in your life.
- Sit quietly for three minutes and pray or listen to Christian music, read Scripture, etc.

After three minutes of spending time with God, record how you feel, what He said to you, what He lifted off you, etc. _____

_____

_____

Journal your stresses, sins, circumstances, fears, desires, and problems on a daily basis. This allows God to free your mind from the enemy's strongholds and the world's temptations. After journaling, record at least one verse of Scripture at the end so that you will always have the voice of God to stand on.

God longs to de-stress your life and restructure your world everyday. May you be blessed as you allow Him to work in your world.

Below is a list of other ways to de-stress your life. If you feel monotonous repeating the above system, change to some of the suggestions below:

- Get out of the stress by helping someone else in need.
- Get your mind on the promises of God.
- Get somewhere quiet and call a friend or mentor with whom you can talk and pray with.
- Walk outside or out of the situation and just breathe slow breaths, refocusing on what really matters.

Chapter Two

Examining My World

Instructions for completing this chapter:
   Tools Required: Bible; pen/pencil; highlighter
   Responsibility: Prayer; honesty; filling in your world; completing the chapter

1 Corinthians 11:28-32 *"But let a man examine himself, and so let him eat of that bread, and drink of that cup. For he that eateth and drinketh unworthily, eateth and drinketh damnation to himself, not discerning the Lord's body. For this cause many are weak and sickly among you, and many sleep. For if we would judge ourselves, we should not be judged. ³²But when we are judged, we are chastened of the Lord, that we should not be condemned with the world."*

We have all heard the saying, "One negative word can destroy a thousand words of positivity." Therefore, if that is true and I believe it is, then we have a lot of work to do on ourselves. We are not only the victims of other people's misery and pain. We are also perpetrators of such behavior. **James 4:1** says, *"From whence come wars and fightings among you? come they not hence, even of your lusts that war in your members?"* If you pay close attention to this verse, you will see that it is speaking in the singular and the personal tense. It excludes everyone but you.

When we are hurting and miserable, we tend to blame others. We cannot face the fact that our issues come from within rather than from those around us. Herein lies the reason and the importance of examining ourselves. The Word of God can and will restructure our world, our thinking, our behavior, and our self-confidence. We will see ourselves as Christ sees us and self-examination will become a daily natural act on our behalf. Our main Scripture text teaches us the importance of self-check ups. It tells us that to rid ourselves of misery, pain, and huge voids that plague our lives, we must drink the cup, and eat the bread of self-examination. It also teaches the consequences if we do not judge ourselves. The Scripture says we will bring the chastening of the Lord upon us. God's examination and His findings in our lives can get very frightening. The Scripture text tells us that lack of examination will make us sick, weak, and spiritually defeated. It also states that if we judge ourselves, God will not have to chasten us. God always honors those who know they are not living in total obedience and holiness to Him. As we confess to Him our faults, fears, and shortcomings, He is faithful to love us through them and make our battles and sins lessons rather than failures.

God is trying to teach us in this verse that becoming a *real* Christian in the real world requires you to cleanse yourself from a life of worldliness. The system is as follows:

      Confess   (Admit to God your sins, faults, and failures)

      Learn   (God's ways, apply them, resist worldliness)

      Endure   (Persecutions, rejections, righteous living)

      Abstain   (Fleshly temptations, worldly lusts, peer pressures, satanic subtlety)

      Nourish   (Nurture and feed your mind with the Word of God)

      Separate   (Refrain from those who have negative influence on your life)

      Exhort   (Encourage those who pressure you to join you in cleanliness)

The more we examine our lives, the more we realize that no one is to blame for our misery and pain but satan and ourselves. In the world we live in, it is easy to get trapped in the rat race of everyday life. We focus on what we consider the main responsibilities and somewhere in the shuffle and chaos, we put the Controller, Protector, and Lover of our soul on the back burner. Let's examine ourselves to see where God is in our world by answering the following questions.

Do I find myself wanting what others have? _____

_____

Is what others think about me an issue? _____

_____

If God came today, would I be found faithful? _____

_____

If I had to reveal my world, what would it look like? _____

_____

Am I happy in my world? _____

_____

How does my world affect those who have to live with and around me? _____

_____

    This list of questions could go on and on, but I think we get the picture by now. The Word of God has this to say in **Romans 12:1-3**, *"I beseech you therefore, brethren, by the mercies of God, that ye present your bodies a living sacrifice, holy, acceptable unto God, which is your reasonable service. And be not conformed to this world: but be ye transformed by the renewing of your mind, that ye may prove what is that good, and acceptable, and perfect, will of God. For I say, through the grace given unto me, to every man that is among you, not to think of himself more highly than he ought to think; but to think soberly, according as God hath dealt to every man the measure of faith."* Does the bread you are eating and the cup you are drinking reflect the life of Christ? If not, the Word of God has just taught us that it should.

    God's plan for and definition of your world is probably completely opposite of your definition. This is why His Word exhorts us to *"...be not conformed to this world."* This statement brings us to another set of questions.

What is your definition of conforming? _____

_____

Do you feel that you have conformed to the standards of this present world system? If yes, please explain the areas in which you feel you have conformed.

_____

_____

Do you understand the definition of being transformed? _____ If yes, write your definition here. _____

_____

_____

How often do you read and study the Word of God? _____

_____

Do you understand the only way to be transformed is to absorb and live the truths of God's Word? _____

_____

Do you know without a doubt that you are saved? _____

_____

Do you ever doubt your salvation? _____

_____

Can you list one thing in your life that you know easily distracts you from living the way God would have you to live? _____

_____

Are there one or more particular habits in your life that Satan uses as strongholds that make you feel that you fail God as a Christian? _____

List them here. _____

_____

_____

As you have answered these questions, you have examined and judged yourself. You are now allowing God to transform your world into His will for His glory. As you allow God to transform you, there are some things that you need to see about yourself. I am listing them below. Be honest with yourself as you read them because this is your beginning point of allowing God to help you.

- Do you love drama (A Drama Queen - trouble always has to be stirring in your life)?
- Do you have a problem being real? Or do you find it easier to be superficial?
- Do you have a problem controlling the tongue?
- Do you have a problem controlling your temper?
- Do you have a problem controlling your behavior?

This is why you were created - for the honor, praise, and glory of God. **1 Corinthians 11:31-32** says, *"For if we would judge ourselves, we should not be judged. But when we are judged, we are chastened of the Lord, that we should not be condemned with the world."* As we judge ourselves, God corrects and disciplines us with love which creates within us a new desire to restructure our lives in a way that is pleasing to Him. As God breaks down the strongholds of our flesh and satan, we become motivated and stirred within to live for and love Jesus Our Savior.

In this chapter, we will review the contents, actions, and effects of our world.

Reviewing the Contents

1 Bob 2:15-17 *"Love not the world, neither the things that are in the world. If any man love the world, the love of the Father is not in him. For all that is in the world, the lust of the flesh, and the lust of the eyes, and the pride of life, is not of the Father, but is of the world. And the world passeth away, and the lust thereof: but he that doeth the will of God abideth for ever."*

We learn from this Scripture text that the main component of our world should be the love of the Father. Therefore, the content of our world should be built upon the love of God shed abroad in our hearts. If we love the things of this world more than we love God, then we have some major work to do. We must restructure our lives in accordance to the will of God so that we can once again feel God's presence, pray with power, receive joy, witness, and live in the security of our salvation.

Our problem with living the Christian life is we have allowed the cares, pleasures, and popular opinions to supersede our intimacy with Jesus Christ. We have grown to literally love the things of this world more than we do God. This is why we feel our lives are twisted and out of shape to the point of no return. We are fulfilling **2 Timothy 3:1-5** which says, *"This know also, that in the last days perilous times shall come. For men shall be lovers of their own selves, covetous, boasters, proud, blasphemers, disobedient to parents, unthankful, unholy, Without natural affection, trucebreakers, false accusers, incontinent, fierce, despisers of those that are good, Traitors, heady, highminded, lovers of pleasures more than lovers of God; Having a form of godliness, but denying the power thereof: from such turn away."* The contents of today's world are listed for us right here:

Perilous Times
Lovers of own selves
Covetous
Boasters
Proud
Blasphemers (rejecters of the Holy Spirit)
Disobedient
Unthankful
Unholy
Without natural affection
Trucebreakers

False accusers
Incontinent
Fierce
Despisers of good
Traitors
Heady
High minded
Lovers of pleasures more than lovers of God
Form of godliness
Denying God's power

46

We must understand that this list was given to a body of believers as a warning. It warns all of us to not become victims to this lifestyle. Do not allow your world to contain these contents. How many of you reading this has already realized that to some degree this is you? Are you guilty of just one of these? I think in all honesty we would all have to answer yes.

Below, you will find an empty circle. Imagine this is your world and put your name on the center line in the middle of the circle. Take just a few moments and honestly fill in the contents of how your world is played out day by day. Begin with the moment you get out of the bed and end with the time you get into bed, taking into consideration the amount of time you spend on each activity that occupies your world. An example and the contents of someone else's world that went through this mentoring system will follow. It will help you understand how to get started filling in the contents of your world.

Filling In Your World

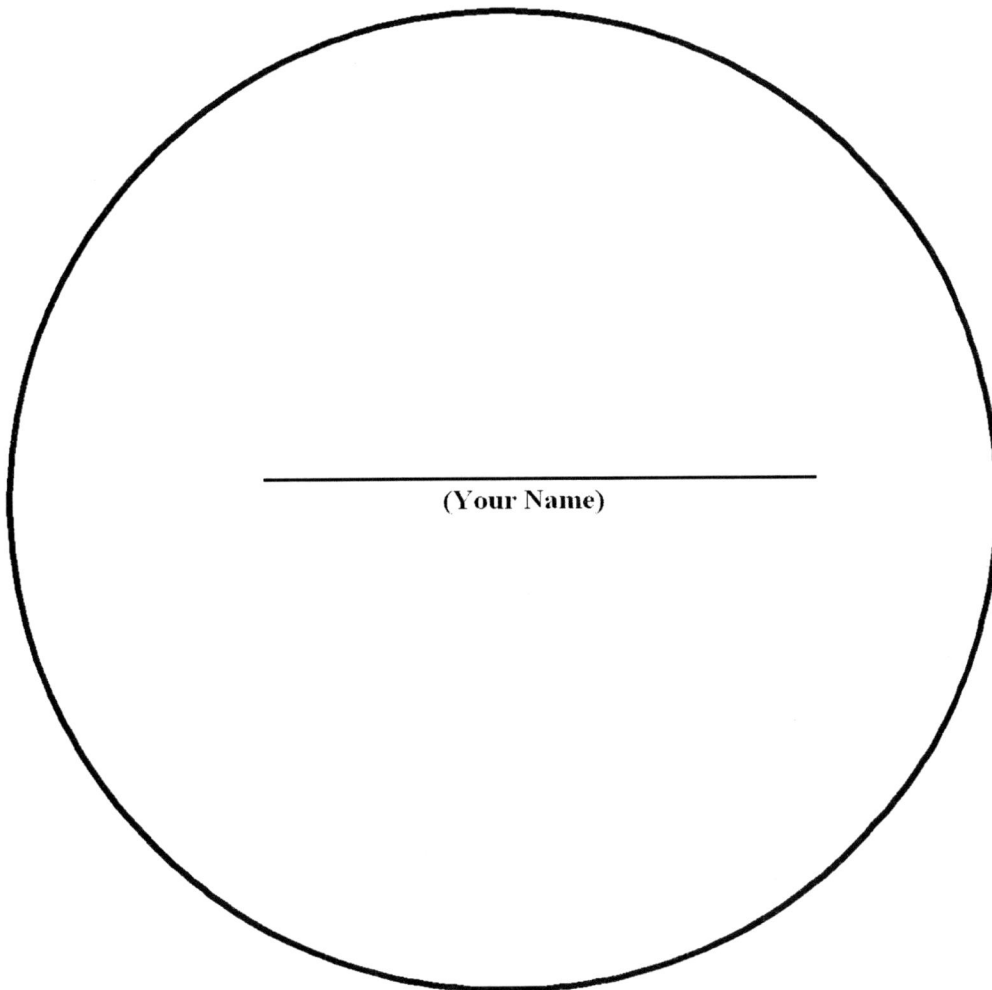

(Your Name)

Example of a Seventeen Year Old's World

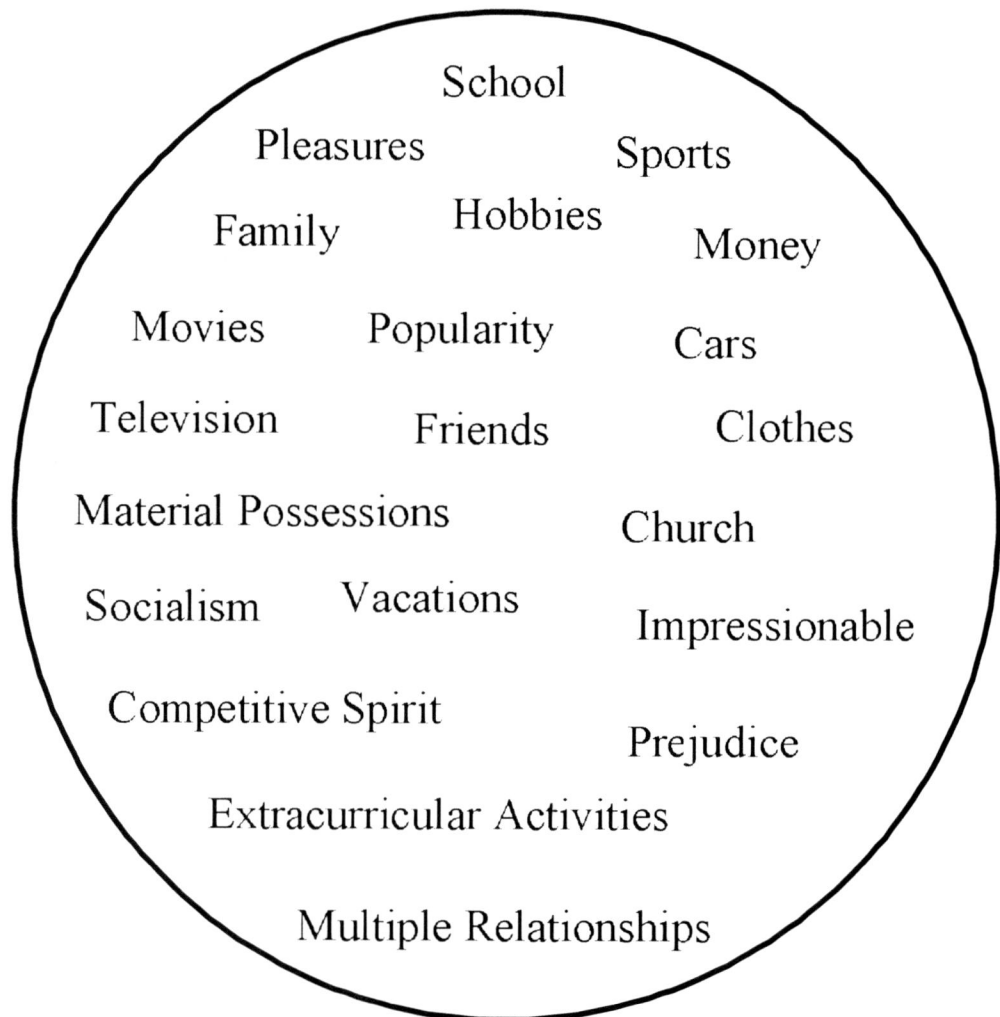

School

Pleasures   Sports

Family   Hobbies   Money

Movies   Popularity   Cars

Television   Friends   Clothes

Material Possessions   Church

Socialism   Vacations   Impressionable

Competitive Spirit   Prejudice

Extracurricular Activities

Multiple Relationships

As you compare the two worlds, can you detect the differences in your priorities versus the priorities of the other person's world? Are they similar? Would you say you live a completely different set of morals than the other person? Or maybe you share the same morals but you have different values?

Pie- Graphing Your World Based on a 24- Hour Day

Refer back to the world that you filled in. The only person that knows how much time is spent on each activity that occupies your world is yourself. Therefore, I challenge you to create a pie graph of your world on the next page based on the amount of time you put in to each activity, reiterating that your world should begin with the moment you get out of bed and end with the moment you go to bed. This graph should reveal to you what percentage of your day is filled with self, world, family, school/college, friends, intimate companions, habits, etc.

Make this fun. Be sure you get some bright crayons and make your pie graph creative. When it is all over, you may need a good laugh. **Matthew 6:33** says, *"But seek ye first the kingdom of God, and his righteousness; and all these things shall be added unto you."*

Example Pie Graph

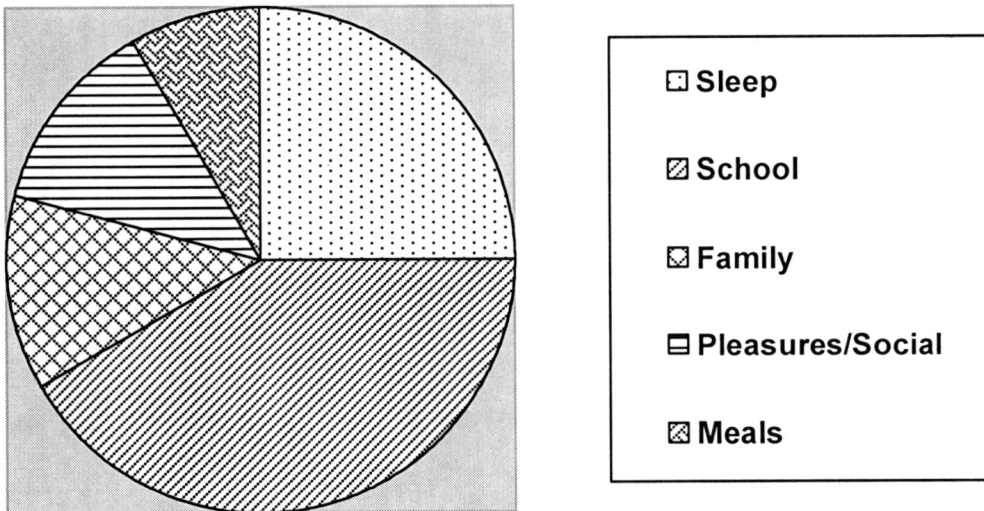

☐ Sleep

☒ School

☒ Family

☐ Pleasures/Social

☒ Meals

Notice in this pie graph example that church, God, and study time are nowhere to be found. The latest statistics prove that the majority of young people leave God out of their daily lives except on Sundays. To make matters worse, the statistics tell us that parents do not enforce the rule that their children should attend church with them as a family or even reverence God as their authority.

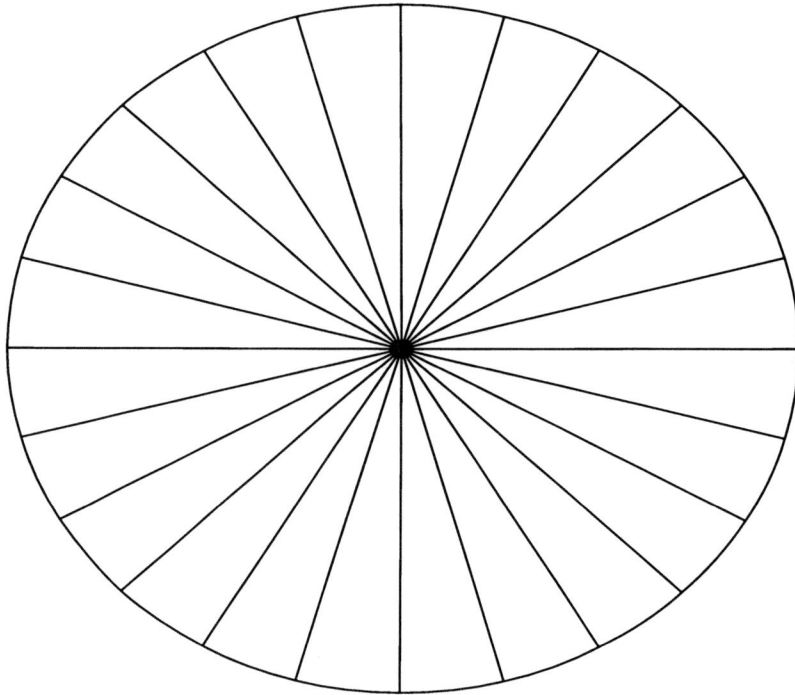

In the pie chart above, there are 24 sections. Each section represents 1 hour of the day.

Color the number of sections that correspond to the number of hours you spend each day on each activity of your daily life. For example, if you sleep for 6 hours per day, color in 6 sections on the chart.

Use a different color for each activity to maximize the effectiveness of this chart. **Be sure to note what activity each color represents.** Once you have colored in all 24 sections, carefully examine what really makes up your day. This chart should help put your life into perspective.

Let's look at the worlds of some other young people who went through this mentoring system. As we review their priorities, let's take a look at the shape of their world and how long they stayed in the mentoring class.

GOD

Family   Church

School   Home Life

Bible Study

Priorities   Goals & Desires

Notice the change

Was not completing assignments

Deception

Accusing friends of betrayal

Excessive spending

Lying to others

Drinking/Drugs

Pre-marital sex

Making fun of others

Bored with

church

This person was not willing to turn their life completely over to God. They lied to me about their true priorities. Although they listed God at the top, they were not sincere with God. Today, this person is depressed, out in the world, and their life is filled with sin. Their bad choices have brought great consequences. When we are only willing to go so far with God, we will reap what we sow. Notice that the change occurred while this person was professing that God was first in their life. The way you live and what you profess to be as a Christian to those around you affects more than just you. You may deceive others, but you cannot deceive God. This person's world imploded, then exploded, and has led to destruction to this very day. Their parents are being disrespected, stolen from, and have no trust in their child.

This next world started out with good intentions. Try to detect what went wrong and when it went wrong.

GOD

Family

Church

Goals & Desires

Popularity   Money   Friends

School

Prayer time   Priorities

Notice the change

Gradually stopped praying and studying

Desires changed

Temptation overtook them   Family friction

Social opinion prevailed

Lust destroyed testimony

Desires shifted from

God to the world

This person truly wanted to love God. They were striving to overcome the lust of their flesh and to grow in their relationship with the Lord. They were faithful to do their study and to apply themselves to the mentoring system. I was amazed at what God was doing in this young person's life. Then one day they came in totally different. Satan had attacked them mentally and fleshly and their desires had changed. This person went from finding their companionship in Christ and family to finding it in someone who was not even a Christian. Their desire for God disappeared. Where are they today? Still out in the world looking for love in all the wrong people and places. This young adult is still trying to find themselves.

Based on the few worlds we have looked at, we would have to conclude that if we are not completely devoted to loving God and living our life for Him, our world will have to be restructured. This brings us to the next subject of this chapter which requires us to change our actions.

Changing Our Actions

Galatians 1: 10 *"For do I now persuade men, or God? or do I seek to please men? for if I yet pleased men, I should not be the servant of Christ."*

I noticed in all the worlds we reviewed everyone's was out of kilter (out of order) somewhere. They all started out with good intentions or thinking their world was doing okay. They thought they were pleasing to God or at least alright in the sight of God.

Most of them made remarks such as "I am a daughter/son", "I go to Church on a regular basis", "I read my Bible every week", "I do good deeds for others", "I'm dependable", "I'm faithful to my parents and family", and "I'm a good person". I could go on and on with the remarks I have heard. However, these actions are not what shape our worlds into lives that produce productive, peaceable young Christians. These actions are our God given responsibilities that we are to perform on a daily basis. These are our duties, not favors, to God.

I also noticed that in most of the worlds, there was a sense of impressing others or keeping the same lifestyle as our peers. This led to remarks such as "It takes both of my parents working so that I can have the same things as my other peers", "My title requires me to live a certain standard", "I do not want to be considered an outcast", "I have to participate in a certain amount of socialism to keep my reputation", "I have to do whatever it takes to fit in", "I have to go out with my friends after school hours". All of these actions must be changed and/or re-evaluated if you are ever going to have a personal relationship with God, a stress-free life, a stable home environment, healthy relationships, and a well rounded world.

Paul states in our Scripture text that we are not to please man. If we do, how can we be the servant of Christ? This statement is coming from someone who had it all and lost it all for the sake of Jesus Christ. This man had restructured his world to please the Heavenly Father. In his heart, no one else mattered. Paul had lived in the world of pleasing man and it got him nowhere. He had sat on thrones and lived in palaces. He had been in political seats and governed the Jewish people. However, he was dethroned and disowned the moment he became a born again believer.

When our actions change, our relationship with God will also change. If our actions change for the world, we will stray farther from God. If our actions change for God, we will draw closer to God and He will draw nearer to us. The less we seek to please man and the world, the more pleasing to God we will become. We will take on a servant's heart and God will be able to use us for His glory. The beauty of all of this is that we will want to be used. We will not want any part of the world. We will be like Paul. We will restructure our world and change our actions to the likeness of Christ. We will fight the good fight and we will stay on course.

Let's look at someone's world that stayed on course in their mentoring system. In this person's world, I noticed four things that kept them on course. They were sincere, honest, desperate, and ready and willing to do whatever it took to have a right relationship with God. From the very first day they walked into my office until this very day, they changed their actions and it has been honored by the Lord.

This was the person's world when they first started the program. As this person's mentor, I rated the contents of this world on a scale of 1 – 10. Even though she had God at the top, notice the rating on God.

(7) God

(8) Family
- Parents
- Siblings
- Grandparents
- Step parents
- Church Family

(1) School
- Academics
- Sports
- School activities

(10) I had to make this person a category for herself because. She had no hope as a young teenager. She didn't think that God could love her. We had to rearrange her thinking.

(9) Spiritual
- Bible Study Time (>30 min/day; some days none)
- Prayer Life - not same as it used to be
- Feel like roller coaster ride - up and down
- Failed God in the past - He can't use me now
- No joy

My Life In General

(2) Problematic Issues
- Low self esteem
- Striving for popularity
- Peer pressure
- Rrelationships
- Resisting worldly temptations

(3) Finances
- Underpriviledged
- Could not afford name brands
- Had to work & go to school

(5) Quite (Me) Time
- Not much for just me

(4) Spiritual desire
(only desires; was not at fruition at this time)

(6) Friends
- Didn't have many because of family's finances

I will tell you based on the priority factor that anyone should be able to figure out this world is the world of a struggling young teenager. How can you tell? She placed herself and time for herself at the bottom of the list. Girls have a tendency to do that. She was doing all God created her to do as a daughter, student, and employee, but what about her relationship with God? In her mind, all of these things were good, but she realized there was a void in her life. She realized God wanted an intimate relationship with her and that He had to be top priority in her world. She stayed true to the program, restructured her world according to God's will, and the rest of her world fell into its proper order. It took time, perseverance, set-backs, and some hurdle jumping, but changing her actions was very effective. She experienced a permanent change as a Christian. Let's turn the page and look at her world as she lives it today. Notice the things that moved out of her world and the new things that became a part of her world.

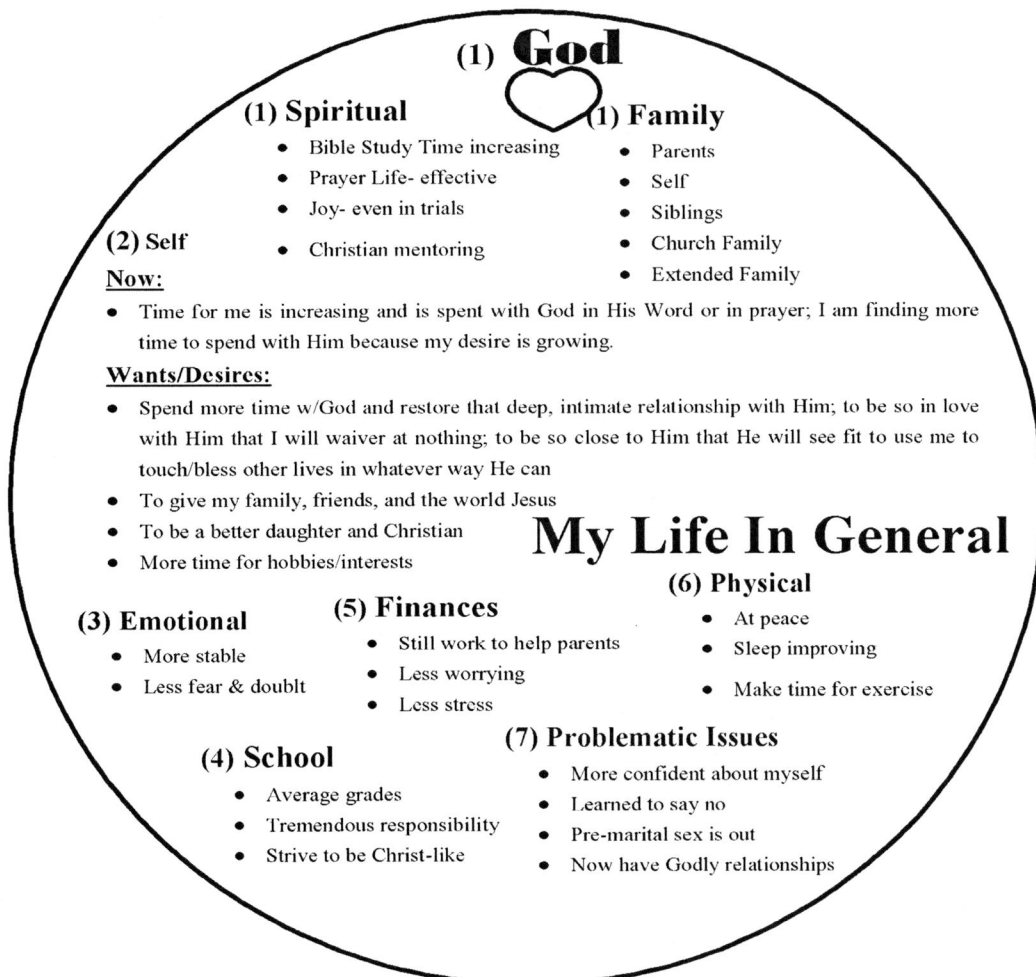

(1) God

(1) Spiritual
- Bible Study Time increasing
- Prayer Life- effective
- Joy- even in trials
- Christian mentoring

(1) Family
- Parents
- Self
- Siblings
- Church Family
- Extended Family

(2) Self
Now:
- Time for me is increasing and is spent with God in His Word or in prayer; I am finding more time to spend with Him because my desire is growing.

Wants/Desires:
- Spend more time w/God and restore that deep, intimate relationship with Him; to be so in love with Him that I will waiver at nothing; to be so close to Him that He will see fit to use me to touch/bless other lives in whatever way He can
- To give my family, friends, and the world Jesus
- To be a better daughter and Christian
- More time for hobbies/interests

My Life In General

(3) Emotional
- More stable
- Less fear & doublt

(5) Finances
- Still work to help parents
- Less worrying
- Less stress

(6) Physical
- At peace
- Sleep improving
- Make time for exercise

(4) School
- Average grades
- Tremendous responsibility
- Strive to be Christ-like

(7) Problematic Issues
- More confident about myself
- Learned to say no
- Pre-marital sex is out
- Now have Godly relationships

This person had come to the end of herself and wanted a real relationship with God. She wanted to be effective in the lives of those who lived with her, came in contact with her, and especially those whom she might could lead to Jesus. The things outside of her world are no longer an issue. Notice her God, Family, and Spiritual categories – the three became one. She's now at a scale of 1 – 7. God has honored her faithfulness. She is becoming spiritually mature.

You may be thinking right now, "How can I change my actions or behavior now? Isn't it too late for me to turn my world around?" My friend, with God it is never too late to change. God is the power within you to make the change. **2 Corinthians 5:17** says, *"Therefore if any man be in Christ, he is a new creature: old things are passed away; behold, all things are become new."* When Christ entered into you an eternal change took place. What you do with that change is your responsibility. God created us with a free will. Eve is a great example. She was told not to eat of the fruit but was influenced by an evil power. Through her free will she chose to eat. Her action brought sin's curse upon the whole world. Thank God for the action of Jesus Christ who chose to hang on a cross to reverse the actions of Adam and Eve.

Unlike Eve, you must examine your actions. What are you doing with your free will? How are you behaving as a child of the King? Do your actions speak holiness or worldliness? **1 Timothy 2:9-15** *"In like manner also, that women adorn themselves in modest apparel, with shamefacedness and sobriety; not with broided hair, or gold, or pearls, or costly array; But (which becometh women professing godliness) with good works. Let the woman learn in silence with all subjection. But I suffer not a woman to teach, nor to usurp authority over the man, but to be in silence. For Adam was first formed, then Eve. And Adam was not deceived, but the woman being deceived was in the transgression. Notwithstanding she shall be saved in childbearing, if they continue in faith and charity and holiness with sobriety."* Based on this scripture, as a young/single Christian lady, does your world reflect a lady who dresses modestly and sets the example for the other young girls who may be watching your life to dress appropriately? It is not a sin to wear jewelry and makeup or to dress trendy, as long as your body is covered and your dress speaks volumes of righteousness and modesty. We as young women need to show a lot less cleavage, and a lot more coverage! You must remember that God created you to be a lady of example in a world that holds no morals or standards of righteousness any longer. If we do not stand as real Christians making a difference, even with our apparel, then we can become stumbling blocks to an even younger generation that is not the church of tomorrow, but the church of today. My friends, I do not believe there is a church of tomorrow because I believe we are in the last days. This is the last generation, so let's stop making someone else responsible. Are you condoning immodesty by purchasing clothing like your friends wear because of the peer pressure you are under? Are you being a disciplinarian based on the Word of God? I have learned over the years of mentoring that most of our young people had rather the parents make the decision of what to wear so they will not fall under the peer pressure of wearing something that makes them uncomfortable, just to feel accepted. When parents make the decision for you, it not only frees you of what your peers think, but it also makes you feel loved and cared for by your parents. By making that decision, you are actually helping to reconstruct your world to one that is pleasing to God.

Are you doing all the things that God requires you to do in fulfilling your duties and responsibilities, yet you find there is still a void? Your void is an intimate relationship with Jesus Christ. You must go back and review your world. What changes do you need to make that will fill your life with Jesus? What part of your world could you rearrange that would allow you and God time together - time to pray, study, worship, serve, and love others? You were created to find joy in these things, not in the things of the world that distract you and stress you out. The Bible teaches us that the things of the world are only temporary and will pass away. **Matthew 6:19-21** says, *"Lay not up for yourselves treasures upon earth, where moth and rust doth corrupt, and where thieves break through and steal: But lay up for yourselves treasures in heaven, where neither moth nor rust doth corrupt, and where thieves do not break through nor steal: For where your treasure is, there will your heart be also."*

Listed below are a few more things the world will steal from you:
- Healthy relationships
- Desire to succeed
- Your self-confidence
- Happiness
- Security
- Peace
- Friendships
- Contentment

The enemy seeks to steal your joy by feeding you the treasures of this world. If he can change your thoughts from God to yourself or the world, then he has you distracted from loving God. This brings us to the final subject of this chapter.

Realizing the Effects

If satan can get you focused on the effects the world has had on you, such as stress, your troubles, your wants, even your success or accomplishments, your rejections, your past, your failures etc., you will feel like you can never change. Satan will have you feeling one of two ways. You will feel either that the world has been too good to you to change now or that it has been too hard on you to change now.

The decision is yours. God wants to change your life to one you will not even recognize. How bad do you want a relationship with the Lover of your soul? Are you to the point that you can't fight the battles anymore? Are you haunted by your past? Are you depressed or hurting? Perhaps you are very successful but still feel an emptiness? My friend, God can reverse the effects of your life. He can take what you see as failure and use it as testimony and fruitfulness for His kingdom work.

If you are realizing there has to be more to life than what you have experienced or are experiencing, then you are ready for God to restructure your world. You are ready for God to be the center of your life above all others. That is His will for your life and it comes with blessings and benefits that will see you through the hardest of times. You will know without a doubt that He is your ultimate counselor that never leaves you. His Word will be your guide book and His voice in your darkest hour. He will be your world and nothing will be able to shake it. **Isaiah 9:6** describes Him like this, *"For unto us a child is born, unto us a son is given: and the government shall be upon his shoulder: and his name shall be called Wonderful, Counsellor, The mighty God, The everlasting Father, The Prince of Peace."*

Now that we have come to know who God wants to be in our lives, let's examine where we are with the effects of the past so that we can live in His wonderful peace. You see, from God's perspective everything from this moment back is the past. You are starting with a clean slate from this moment forward. The first key to making God your ultimate counselor is found in **1 Bob 1:9.** It says, *"If we confess our sins, he is faithful and just to forgive us our sins, and to cleanse us from all unrighteousness."* Confession is the key. You must tell God everything that hurts you, makes you bitter, your thoughts, your longings and desires, and your past, especially those things you cannot let go of.

Does your past still hold you back from serving God? _____

If yes, how often do you think about your past? _____

_____

How does it affect the way you feel about yourself? _____

_____

How does it affect how you socialize with others? _____

_____

Have you confessed your past to God? _____

_____

Have you confided in someone else as a mentor? _____

_____

Do you want to be rid of the past? _____

_____

Do you believe that God can free you of your past? _____

_____

If this particular section of this study is not for you, do you know someone who it could benefit? If yes, would you consider being their mentor by sharing this with them?

If you have overcome the effects of your world and are living for God, you can help someone else restructure their world into the likeness of Christ. **Galatians 6:2-3** says, *"Bear ye one another's burdens, and so fulfil the law of Christ. For if a man think himself to be something, when he is nothing, he deceiveth himself."* Let's move on now to the next chapter that brings us to our present world and the life we are living.

Teen Connection
by Brooke Cason

Resisting Peer Pressure

James 4:7 *"Submit yourselves therefore to God. Resist the devil, and he will flee from you."*

It does not matter how young or how old you are, at some point in time you have to deal with peer pressure. I come into contact with peer pressure almost daily in some form. Let's define peer pressure. We have to break it down into two parts. Peer is defined as a friend, an equal (someone who you see as being equal to you), or a colleague (someone you work with or go to school with.) Pressure is a force, something heavy, or something that weighs you down. Now let's think together. Peer pressure is when a friend or acquaintance forces you or tries to force you to do something you know is wrong. Peer pressure comes in many forms, such as, gossiping, drinking, drugs, sex, brand of clothes you wear, and whatever else you do to try to fit in. You may put someone down or be put down because your family may not have a lot of money, or you may come from a home with an alcoholic or drug addict parent. Those are things you or the person you are making fun of cannot help. These are pressures from our peers. You don't have to be ashamed of not wearing name brand clothes or not having a lot of money. Those are material possessions. God does not look at that. He looks at your heart. You do not have to be "cool" to fit in. God has called us to be "a peculiar people."

Another type of peer pressure we come into contact with is "adult peer pressure." What do I mean by adult peer pressure? Let me explain. I had friends whose parents would buy them as much alcohol as they wanted. They would always ask me, "What kind do you want?" My answer was always "I don't want anything tonight" instead of what I should have said: "I don't drink because it's not right in the eyes of God and I'm not old enough anyway." It is okay to resist the temptations instead of falling to them. God will make a way of escape. **1 Corinthians 10:13 says,** *"There hath no temptation taken you but such as is common to man: but God is faithful, who will not suffer you to be tempted above that ye are able; but will with the temptation also make a way to escape, that ye may be able to bear it."*

Another example of adult peer pressure that I hear a lot about is teachers, church leaders, family members, etc. making passes at young people. This disgusts me, but it happens all the time. I will give you an example of a young person who came to us for mentoring. This person's "adult peer" started telling them that their companion didn't love them anymore, and they needed to be loved. They came to them slowly like satan does. The next thing that happened was the adult started sending this child text messages. Of course this child got scared. This person was coming home crying everyday. This person knew if they told their parents they would go to the school board and the adult would lose their job. The child did not want their fellow classmates to be mad at them for turning the adult in because the other classmates liked this person in authority. It went on and on until it scared the child enough that they told their parents. The parents then went to the school board and addressed the situation. Of course, the adult lost their job. That was the right thing for them to do. But now, the child wants to know how to forgive themselves. They did nothing wrong. They just happened to be the victim. They did not flaunt themselves at the adult; the adult just picked this person out of a crowd. Sounds like satan. That is how he works. This person did not do anything wrong. There is no reason for them to blame themselves!

Satan is always looking for a way to creep into your life and make you do things that are wrong (sin). If you will turn to God for direction and guidance, He will make a way of escape for you. The choice is yours. Will you choose God or will you choose satan? It is not Godly to live under the pressures of others. You do not have to please those around you. You should concentrate on what is pleasing to God most of all and then what is pleasing to your parents. Making fun of people is not pleasing to God. It could happen to you at any time. You and your family could lose everything you have by morning. Be thankful today for what God has blessed you with, and pray for those who are not as fortunate as you. Do not allow your peers to conform you to their ways. Do not allow adults to take advantage of you and scare you. You do not have to be scared to tell your parents what somebody has done to you. Your parents will go out of their way to protect you from harm. God does not honor peer pressure. Do not be the victim or the instigator!

Are you the victim of peer pressure?_____

If so what kind? _____

_____

_____

_____

_____

_____

Are you the instigator of peer pressure? _____

If so, why? _____

_____

_____

Are you constantly worried about fitting in? _____

Do you mind being peculiar for Christ? _____

What are you willing to do to bring others to Christ? _____

_____

_____

_____

_____

_____

_____

_____

_____

_____

_____

_____

_____

_____

_____

_____

_____

_____

_____

_____

_____

_____

_____

_____

De-stressing Your Life

Below is a system that will help you restructure your life on a daily basis. Follow this system when you feel you are overwhelmed, stressed, and need to feel the presence of God in your life.

Define the stress and record it below. _____

_____

_____

Explain how it makes you feel inside. _____

_____

_____

Describe how you respond to the stress. For example, do you feel anger, fear, nervous, anxious, etc? _____

_____

_____

Who or what provoked you? _____

_____

_____

You have just dealt with and confronted your stress and its issues by answering the above questions. Now, let's free ourselves, clear our minds, and give it all to God with the following steps:

- Focus on God and His goodness by listing one issue of praise to God for today.
- Take a moment and thank Him for the day and the fact that He helped you through it.
- Acknowledge Him as your Ultimate Guide, Helper, and Comforter in your life.
- Sit quietly for three minutes and pray or listen to Christian music, read Scripture, etc.

After three minutes of spending time with God, record how you feel, what He said to you, what He lifted off you, etc. _____

_____

_____

Journal your stresses, sins, circumstances, fears, desires, and problems on a daily basis. This allows God to free your mind from the enemy's strongholds and the world's temptations. After journaling, record at least one verse of Scripture at the end so that you will always have the voice of God to stand on.

God longs to de-stress your life and restructure your world everyday. May you be blessed as you allow Him to work in your world.

Below is a list of other ways to de-stress your life. If you feel monotonous repeating the above system, change to some of the suggestions below:

- Get out of the stress by helping someone else in need.
- Get your mind on the promises of God.
- Get somewhere quiet and call a friend or mentor with whom you can talk and pray with.
- Walk outside or out of the situation and just breathe slow breaths, refocusing on what really matters.

Journal your thoughts and feelings. _____

_____

_____

_____

_____

_____

_____

_____

_____

_____

_____

_____

Research and record Scriptures that help you work through your thoughts and feelings.

_____

_____

_____

_____

_____

_____

_____

_____

_____

_____

_____

_____

Chapter Three

Rearranging My World

Instructions for completing this chapter:

Tools Required:	Bible; A study book such as *A New Desire, A Victorious Christian Life, It is Finished,* or *Made Over* by Brenda J. Robinson, or another study book of your preference
Responsibility:	Prayer; honesty; filling in your world; completing the chapter

Matthew 6:33 *"But seek ye first the kingdom of God, and his righteousness; and all these things shall be added unto you."*

*I*n chapter two, we examined ourselves. We reviewed our lives and come to grips with the things that made up our world. We reviewed the contents and realized the affects those contents had on our lives. It is now time to make a move.

God wants to rearrange some things about your life that can break strongholds, free you from your past, cleanse your heart, and transform your mind. If you remember in chapter two we spoke about our worlds being out of kilter. Well, the word rearrange means to change the order or position of something or someone. Synonyms for the word rearrange are reorganize and reshuffle. As Christians, it is time that we gain victory by reorganizing our world. Being a *real* Christian in the real world requires you to repent.

*R*epent   (Turn to God. He will turn you from sin and the other things that causes disorganization in your life.)

*E*xchange (Exchange old habits that are displeasing to God for righteous behavior.)

*P*ersevere (A real Christian is never defeated or intimidated by the real world.)

*E*xpect   (Expect God to renovate things that need to be changed in your life.)

*N*eed   (Always need God. When you think you can do it on your own, you have left repentance and turned to the world.)

*T*rust   (Place your trust in the Word of God and the voice of God. He will direct your path.)

In chapter two, we saw the world of a young Christian that was sincere, honest, desperate, and ready and willing to do whatever it took to have a right relationship with God. As you can see, her world as she began the mentoring system was consumed by worldly priorities. As she began studying she began to seek God first in all things. She realized that things of this world are temporal and will pass away. She set her affections from things of this world to things above. As she began spending time with God in His Word and in prayer, she began to see God restructure her world. The worldly possessions, prestige, and popularity that she once put so much time and effort into began to carry less merit for her. She began to lay up treasures in heaven and soon realized that *"where your treasure is, there will your heart be also."* She dealt with past failures, and realized that God has a work for her to do now. Her second world shows that her heart is on God, her spiritual walk, and her family. Her priorities are now on things of God instead of things of this world, and she lives in victory that she had not before experienced. This young woman was so transformed! She stayed true to her study book, *A New Desire Workbook,* and the Word of God.

Her attitude about herself, God, and others changed. This person who was ready to quit school, leave home, and live her way became such a testimony to all those around her whom she once participated in sin with. She became a soul winner and learned to say no to all temptations, because at the age of seventeen, she found true love in Jesus Christ.

Our Present Condition

Again, in chapter two, we took a look at our past and how it has affected our lives. Today, we are going to deal with our present condition and what we need to do to rearrange things to become more pleasing to God.

We know that Jesus tells us to seek Him first. We also know that we are to love others as we love ourselves and we are to forgive if we expect to be forgiven. The problem with applying these specific principles to our lives is that we are so much about self and our problems that it is almost impossible to put God first. We cannot love others because we do not love ourselves; and we certainly cannot forgive others if we refuse to forgive ourselves. Therefore, to deal with our present condition we must first deal with ourselves.

The Bible says in **Luke 6:37-41,** *"Judge not, and ye shall not be judged: condemn not, and ye shall not be condemned: forgive, and ye shall be forgiven: Give, and it shall be given unto you; good measure, pressed down, and shaken together, and running over, shall men give into your bosom. For with the same measure that ye mete withal it shall be measured to you again. And he spake a parable unto them, Can the blind lead the blind? shall they not both fall into the ditch? The disciple is not above his master: but every one that is perfect shall be as his master. And why beholdest thou the mote that is in thy brother's eye, but perceivest not the beam that is in thine own eye?"*

What is this Scripture really saying? It is saying to **deal with yourself!** Do not blame others for your behavior. Do not point fingers at those you love or at God. You must pinpoint the problems that lie deep within you. There you will find your enemy wreaking havoc in your world, your mind, your heart, and your home. The Bible cautions in **1 Peter 5:8** to *"Be sober, be vigilant; because your adversary the devil, as a roaring lion, walketh about, seeking whom he may devour:"*

As we allow the enemy to devour us, we get down on ourselves. We realize that the person who was once happy, full of life, and enjoyed life is now fighting to laugh, love, and give of ourselves as Christ gave Himself for us. We struggle daily just to find one good thing about ourselves. Yet, in **Luke 12:6-7,** Jesus says this about us, *"Are not five sparrows sold for two farthings, and not one of them is forgotten before God? But even the very hairs of your head are all numbered. Fear not therefore: ye are of more value than many sparrows."* He also says in **Psalm 139:17-18** *"How precious also are thy thoughts unto me, O God! how great is the sum of them! If I should count them, they are more in number than the sand: when I awake, I am still with thee."* If Jesus' thoughts are precious toward us, we should rearrange our thoughts about ourselves. Again, we must transform our minds by the reading and studying of God's Word.

Let's rearrange our present condition using the Word of God to counteract the negative for the positive. Do any of the words below fit your world? If yes, use the positive to rearrange your life.

Negative	Positive
Fear	2 Timothy 1:7-8
Low Self Esteem	Colossians 2:6-7
Anger	Ecclesiastes 7:9
Bitterness	Ephesians 4:31-32
The Past	Philippians 3:13
Grief	1 Peter 2:19
Social Status	2 Corinthians 6:17-18
Loneliness	Psalm 27:9-10
Divorce	1 Corinthians 7:8-9
Abuse	Psalm 34:18-19
Depression	Bob 10:10
Oppression	Hebrews 12:1
Misery	Proverbs 15:13
Hatred	Matthew 5:43-44
Jealousy	1 Peter 1:22
Unforgiveness	Colossians 3:13
Fornication	1 Corinthians 10:13
Insecurities	Psalm 138:7-8
Sin	1 Bob 1:9
Faults	Isaiah 26:3-4
Failures	Romans 8:37-39
Rebellion	Hebrews 12:11-15
Addictions	1 Peter 4:1-8
Cruelty	Psalm 37:1-7
Deception	Bob 8:31-36

If any of these represent your present condition, you can counteract them by transforming your mind with the Word of God and other study tools. The Word of God alone will be sufficient for you. However, study tools will keep you on track and help you to know where to go in the Bible to deal with your issues.

From this list you have detected what you need to work on. It should excite you that the enemy can no longer use it as a stronghold in your life. For every negative word that related to you, God has a Scripture to restore you. Your responsibility is to release yourself from the negative and take hold of the Word of God, the truth that will free you from a world of strife.

In the space below, take a few moments to list negatives in your life that may not be on the previous list. Study the Word of God and your study book to find ways to counteract your negatives with something positive.

The negatives in my life	Counteract your negative with Scripture
_____	_____
_____	_____
_____	_____
_____	_____
_____	_____
_____	_____
_____	_____
_____	_____
_____	_____
_____	_____
_____	_____
_____	_____

Now take some time to journal and reflect on what you have learned through your study of the Word of God and the other study tools you have found to be useful.

_____

_____

_____

_____

_____

_____

_____

_____

_____

Once you realize that you are free, you will then move on to setting future goals for yourself.

Future Goals

Philippians 3:13-15 *"Brethren, I count not myself to have apprehended: but this one thing I do, forgetting those things which are behind, and reaching forth unto those things which are before, I press toward the mark for the prize of the high calling of God in Christ Jesus."*

Paul is telling us in this Scripture that even he had present conditions that often hindered him from being and doing all he wanted to for God. In spite of his feelings and his foes, he still made plans for the future. His future was set on seeing his Savior and leading others to Him.

When you come to the realization that God loves you and He only wants for you to love Him in the same way, you too will have goals that will magnify Him. Your goal will be to press on for Jesus. Your goal will be to leave the past behind and build a future that wins souls and edifies the Master. As you work through the issues in your life that have you bound, your goals toward yourself, others, and especially God will take on a new perspective.

There is a great Bible example of someone who had future goals in spite of their odds. This person was Joseph, the son of Jacob. His brothers stripped him of his coat of many colors that his father had just made for him. Their jealousy conspired against him and threw him in a pit, then sold him into Egyptian slavery that landed Joseph in prison where he became an interpreter of Pharaoh's dreams. This landed him second in command in the palace. The point of this story is that Joseph speaks bravely as his goals unfold before his brothers who sought to destroy him as he looked at them and said, *"...Fear not: for am I in the place of God? But as for you, ye thought evil against me; but God meant it unto good, to bring to pass, as it is this day, to save much people alive."*

Joseph's goals about himself and his brothers changed. He kept his heart on God while his goal was the palace. God honored Joseph's heart.

The biggest reason most of us cannot accomplish the goals we set out to achieve is because when we get in situations like Joseph, we fall into the pit of self-pity, the prison of oppression, and we choose to stay there rather than pressing forward toward our exodus. Paul states in our Scripture text that we must forget the things which are behind and reach forth unto those things which are before. I don't know about you, but I have been through enough that I am ready to be like Joseph and Paul. I am ready for the palace life.

If you will keep your heart in Christ, your future goals will look like the goals on the following page:

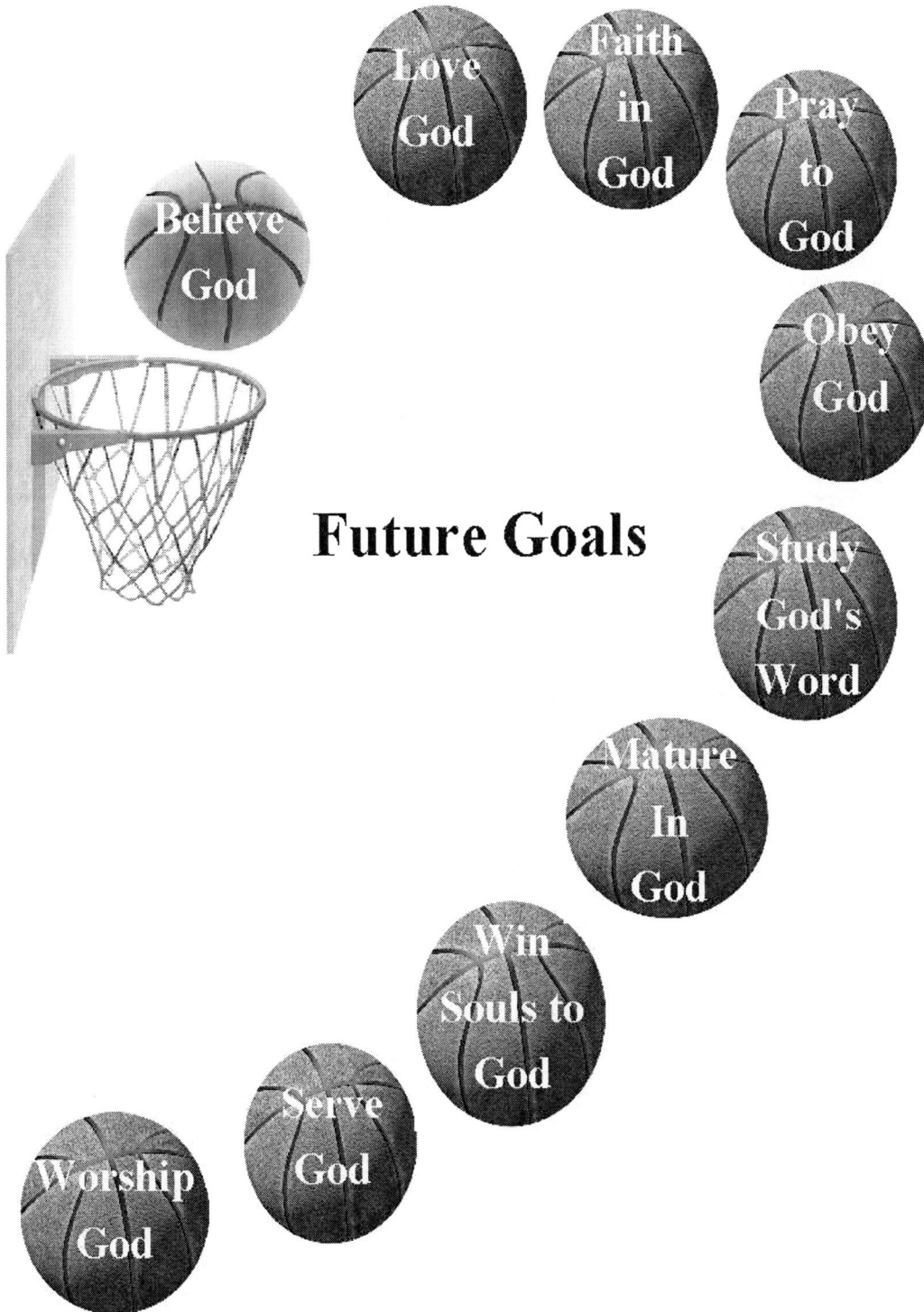

Future Goals

Love God

Faith in God

Pray to God

Believe God

Obey God

Study God's Word

Mature In God

Win Souls to God

Serve God

Worship God

The more you seek God and the more you study His Word, the more of these goals you will accomplish. Strive to study everyday, even if it is only for a few minutes. Let studying your Bible or your workbook be a daily goal in your personal walk with God. He is faithful to speak, if you will allow Him to.

As you seek Him with your whole heart, your whole world will change. You will establish your priorities in accordance to His will.

As you review the future goals, I challenge you to prioritize them in a way in which you feel you can achieve them in accordance with your relationship with God. List them below.

_____

_____

_____

_____

_____

_____

_____

_____

_____

_____

_____

_____

_____

_____

Establishing your Priorities

If you look back at the beginning of this chapter, you are told to *"seek first the kingdom of God"*. If you are doing everything God is telling you to do, then your priorities are already being rearranged. It may not appear that way to you and it may not feel that way right now, but I can assure you that God is doing a new thing in your life. **Isaiah 43:18-19** says, *"Remember ye not the former things, neither consider the things of old. Behold, I will do a new thing; now it shall spring forth; shall ye not know it? I will even make a way in the wilderness, and rivers in the desert."*

The goals you have made for yourself will be one of the tools that will help you establish your priorities. Reviewing the contents of your world as you filled it in in chapter two of this book is another tool that will help you establish your priorities. Reviewing your study book and the notes you have taken will help keep you prioritized; and the Word of God as your weapon will prepare you for whatever lies ahead.

In the space below, reestablish your priorities based on where your spiritual desires are now, compared to where they were when you started this study.

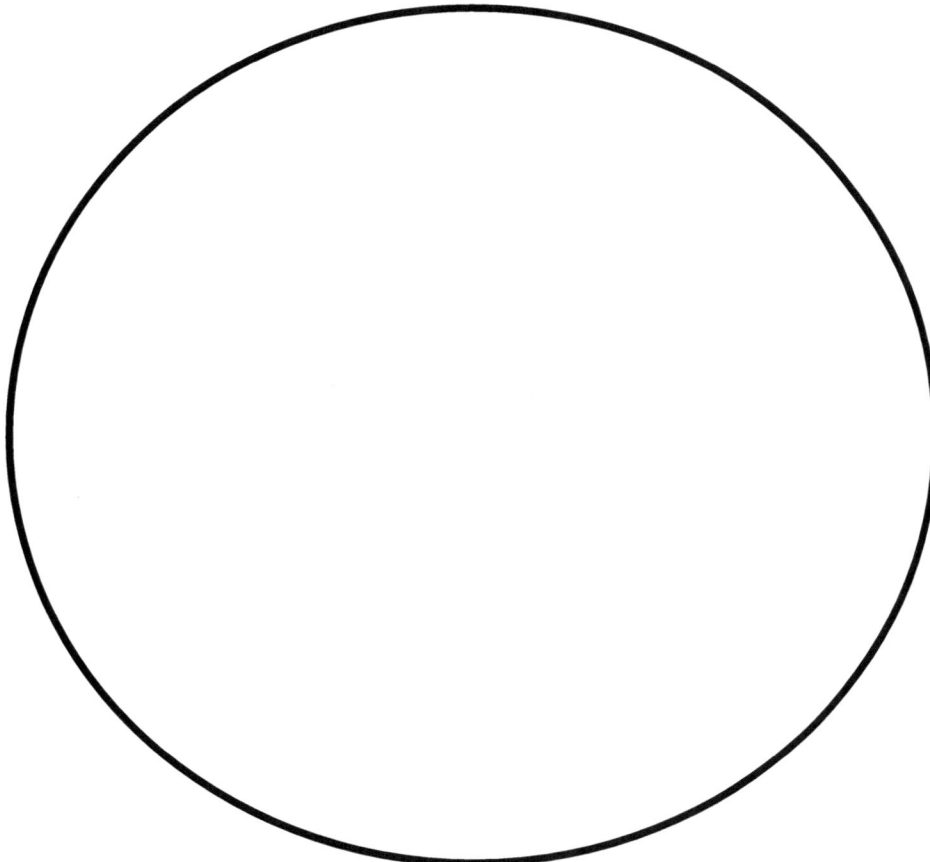

Do you see any differences in your two worlds? _____

If yes, note the differences. _____

_____

_____

_____

_____

Do you find yourself to be more positive? _____

If yes, in what way? _____

_____

_____

_____

_____

Are you struggling with moving forward in some areas of sacrifice? _____

If so, in what areas? _____

_____

_____

_____

_____

Have you reviewed the two worlds in chapter two that destructed? _____

If yes, state your opinion. _____

_____

_____

_____

Do you feel that your world relates better to one of them? _____

If yes, which one and why? _____

_____

_____

_____

Are you allowing God to counsel you by reading and studying your Bible? _____

If yes, record some things He has taught you. _____

_____

_____

_____

_____

_____

_____

_____

_____

_____

_____

Are you doing a study book to help you stay in the Word of God? _____

If yes, list some things you have learned from it. _____

_____

_____

_____

_____

_____

_____

_____

_____

_____

_____

_____

_____

Teen Connection
by Brooke Cason

Be A Peculiar People & Honor Thy Mother & Father

Titus 2:14 *"Who gave himself for us, that he might redeem us from all iniquity, and purify unto himself a peculiar people, zealous of good works."*

As teens living in today's world, we tend to try to find a place to fit in. We want to wear brand name clothes, drive spiced up cars, run with the popular crowd, etc. Our mind is set on worldly possessions and not Heavenly treasures. All these things are great if they do not come between you and God. We fight the battles of peer pressure, self-confidence, acceptance, parental rules, and so much more. It is a hard life.

Where does God fit in? Do you have time for Him? He is a vital part that makes your world go around. Even though you may not sense Him, He is there. He is everywhere at all times. He allows you every breath that you take. What does it mean to be peculiar? It means to be unusual or abnormal. The Scripture text in **Titus 2:14** says that He wants us to be a peculiar people. It is ok to be different, unusual, or abnormal. We do not have to fit in with the rest of the crowd. Running with the crowd might get you into trouble. I know that being different in school did not make me unpopular or not liked. I had a lot of friends. We were all considered to be popular. I am not saying that matters, but to some it does. Just because I was friends with these people did not mean that I did everything that they did. I did not mind being different. Have you ever felt like you were being shameful to your parents or to your "Christian" name because you wanted to fit in with the rest of your friends? I promise you that your friends, if they are true friends, will like you for being different, especially if you are living a life of righteousness. If they make fun of you for being Godly, they were not your true friends to begin with.

You should always think about what you do when you leave home. Do not do anything that you think your parents would not approve of. Do not lie to them about where you are or what you are doing. I promise that they will find out sooner or later. I know when I think back to my teenage years, my father always told me, "What you do when you leave this house reflects on me. Do you want to ruin our family name?" This kept me out of a lot of trouble. I did not want to bring shame on my father. In my life today, I live by the same quote except my every action reflects on my Heavenly Father. People know I am a Christian, and if I reflect evil it gives all "Christians" a bad name. It affects the "whole Christian family." It never mattered how bad I was, my daddy always disciplined me, loved me, and forgave me all at the same time. God is the same way. No matter what sin you have in your life, if you are a born again believer, there will be chastening (correction), love, and forgiveness with confession. He is a loving Father.

There is a command that comes from God found in **Exodus 20:12**. The Scripture says, *"Honour thy father and thy mother: that thy days may be long upon the land which the LORD thy God giveth thee."* What this scripture means is that if we will honor our father and mother then we should live a long life. We should really take this to heart. God expects us to be respectful to our parents. There will be times that our parents will want us to do things that we do not want to do, but we should follow through with their commands because it is what God commands us to do. Our parents are authority over us just like God is the authority over the church. We do not always want to clean our rooms, wear the clothes that they want us to wear, wash the dishes, do other chores, but that is a part of being a child and learning responsibility and respect. Doing what we are told is showing honor to our parents or our authority. We should do the same in school. We will always have someone in authority over us. Even if you are in the highest position in a large corporation, you will still have to answer to someone. In situations where there is really no one else to answer to, remember you still have to answer to God. He is our Supreme Authority. God promises us a long life if we honor our father and mother.

Do you feel like you have brought shame to your family?_____

If so, what did you do and why do you feel like it was shameful? _____

_____

_____

_____

Do you find it hard to forgive yourself for things that you have done? _____

_____

_____

Find a scripture that relates to God's forgiveness and write it here. _____

_____

_____

Do you feel that you show honor to your parents? _____

If not, explain. _____

_____

_____

Are there things that you would change about your relationship with your parents? _____

If yes, list them here. _____

_____

_____

_____

_____

_____

_____

_____

_____

_____

_____

_____

_____

_____

_____

De-stressing Your Life

Below is a system that will help you restructure your life on a daily basis. Follow this system when you feel you are overwhelmed, stressed, and need to feel the presence of God in your life.

Define the stress and record it below. _____

_____

_____

Explain how it makes you feel inside. _____

_____

_____

Describe how you respond to the stress. For example, do you feel anger, fear, nervous, anxious, etc? _____

_____

_____

Who or what provoked you? _____

_____

_____

You have just dealt with and confronted your stress and its issues by answering the above questions. Now, let's free ourselves, clear our minds, and give it all to God with the following steps:

- Focus on God and His goodness by listing one issue of praise to God for today.
- Take a moment and thank Him for the day and the fact that He helped you through it.
- Acknowledge Him as your Ultimate Guide, Helper, and Comforter in your life.
- Sit quietly for three minutes and pray or listen to Christian music, read Scripture, etc.

After three minutes of spending time with God, record how you feel, what He said to you, what He lifted off you, etc. _____

_____

_____

Journal your stresses, sins, circumstances, fears, desires, and problems on a daily basis. This allows God to free your mind from the enemy's strongholds and the world's temptations. After journaling, record at least one verse of Scripture at the end so that you will always have the voice of God to stand on.

God longs to de-stress your life and restructure your world everyday. May you be blessed as you allow Him to work in your world.

Below is a list of other ways to de-stress your life. If you feel monotonous repeating the above system, change to some of the suggestions below:

- Get out of the stress by helping someone else in need.
- Get your mind on the promises of God.
- Get somewhere quiet and call a friend or mentor with whom you can talk and pray with.
- Walk outside or out of the situation and just breathe slow breaths, refocusing on what really matters.

Journal your thoughts and feelings. _____

_____

_____

_____

_____

_____

_____

_____

_____

_____

_____

_____

_____

Research and record Scriptures that help you work through your thoughts and feelings.

_____

_____

_____

_____

_____

_____

_____

_____

_____

_____

_____

_____

_____

Chapter Four

Finding God's Plan

Instructions for completing this chapter:

Tools Required: Bible; A study book such as *A New Desire, A Victorious Christian Life, It is Finished, or Made Over* by Brenda J. Robinson, or another study book of your preference

Responsibility: Prayer; honesty; make decisions; get out of the maze; complete the chapter

Isaiah 55:8-11 *"For my thoughts are not your thoughts, neither are your ways my ways, saith the LORD. For as the heavens are higher than the earth, so are my ways higher than your ways, and my thoughts than your thoughts. For as the rain cometh down, and the snow from heaven, and returneth not thither, but watereth the earth, and maketh it bring forth and bud, that it may give seed to the sower, and bread to the eater: So shall my word be that goeth forth out of my mouth: it shall not return unto me void, but it shall accomplish that which I please, and it shall prosper in the thing whereto I sent it."*

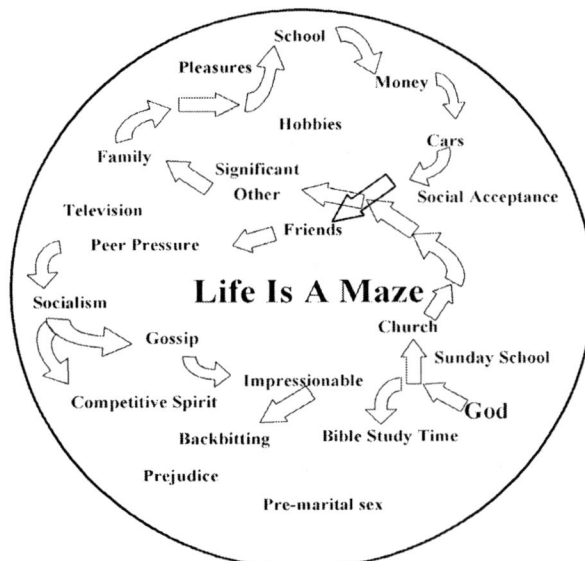

*I*n spite of what we know is right, we are still in the warfare of our flesh and spirit. The enemy and our flesh are pulling us one way, while the Holy Spirit of God is gently leading us toward the path of righteousness. **Psalm 27:11-14** says, *"Teach me thy way, O LORD, and lead me in a plain path, because of mine enemies. Deliver me not over unto the will of mine enemies: for false witnesses are risen up against me, and such as breathe out cruelty. I had fainted, unless I had believed to see the goodness of the LORD in the land of the living. Wait on the LORD: be of good courage, and he shall strengthen thine heart: wait, I say, on the LORD."*

The last two chapters have been painful for us. The fact is that it has forced us to look at our lives from the inside out. We feel we have gone through a whirlwind. I do not know about you, but I feel like I have experienced a hurricane. I feel like my hair is standing straight up, to the side, and lying flat on my head all at the same time. Can you imagine what I look like about right now? I feel like a palm tree bent half over, but praise God I'm still standing. I look like a ship slung up on shore with my sails torn and my boat full of holes ripped by the rocks that it is resting on, but praise God at least it is on the rocks. It could be sunk in the water. You see, we are now at a determining point of total surrender to a life of righteousness or worldliness. In the midst of your maze, you must make some decisions about God and righteousness. **Matthew 6:24** says, *"No man can serve two masters: for either he will hate the one, and love the other; or else he will hold to the one, and despise the other. Ye cannot serve God and mammon."*

The greatest problem with finding God's plan for our life is that we are running around in the world doing worldly things. We are stumbling all over the lust of our flesh, the tactics of satan, worldly principles, and falling into sin. We cannot operate our Christian life based on worldly principles. We must stop running from one worldly thing to another, trying to find God's plan and will for our life. This is why we are not labeled real Christians. On Sundays, we are in church serving the Lord, but through the week, people see us acting just like the world. We are flirting, telling or participating in perverted jokes, drinking and drugs, or allowing perverted language to fall from our mouth. The Lord called us to be a peculiar people. Going to church is not enough to keep us right with God. Perhaps it makes our flesh feel better, but if it is not making us act any better outside of the church, then we are not presenting ourselves as real Christians. We still look like the real world. I just had a young lady who has been a church member all her life, to receive Jesus Christ as her Savior. The very first words she said to me were "I go to church and act like a Christian, and everybody thinks I am. But when I get home, no one would be able to tell me apart from the world." She looked at me and made this statement, "I am lost, miserable with life, I am a person of deception and I want a different life." Can Jesus still use me after this superficial life I have been living?" This was my response, **1 Bob 2:15-17** says, *"Love not the world, neither the things that are in the world. If any man love the* *world, the love of the Father is not in him. For all that is in the world, the lust of the flesh, and the lust of the eyes, and the pride of life, is not of the Father, but is of the world. And the world passeth away, and the lust thereof: but he that doeth the will of God abideth for ever."* Needless to say, they left my office with a whole new outlook on life.

The world is neither the answer nor the place for finding God's plan for your life. Regardless of how successful or unsuccessful you have been, there is only one place to find God's divine plan for your life. The Word of God is that place. You do not have to be a theologian to know His direct plan for "whosoever will". His direct plan for you is that you must be born again, you must be obedient, and you must live by faith:

*F*aith   (Living for and believing in a God whom you have never seen.)

*A*ssurance   (Knowing that regardless of the mistakes you make, He is there
               to make them lessons; and He will love you through them.)

*I*nspiration (Because of who you are in Him, faith will inspire you to do
               things before you see the resources.)

*T*ruth   (Truth is the resource that will help you stand when you are in
               doubt of everyone around you. Truth is the Word of God, and
               truth is the person Jesus Christ.)

*H*ope   (Faith builds hope in a God we've never seen, and our hope
               should only be in Him.)

The principles God gives us of being born again, being obedient, and living by faith are not choices. They are commands for all who serve in the Kingdom of God. Which of these three are you struggling with? Maybe you are moving forward in all three. I pray that you are. God's will for you is to find pleasure in these things and to live a joyous life in Him.

God's plan for every born again believer is to train them up in three areas of righteousness: making Him first; studying His Word; and applying His truths.

Making Him First

It is vitally important to understand the fact that without God first in your life, you will not succeed at anything. Jesus put you before Himself as He hung on Calvary and died for your sin. Therefore, your responsibility is to put Him above all things and all others. You see, finding God's plan for your life is not like getting out and looking for a job. God's plan is made accessible for you and is laid out for you in the pages of the Word of God.

The Word of God says to seek God first; love the Lord with all your heart, soul, and mind; and walk in the Spirit, not in the flesh. Doing all these things is part of making Jesus Christ first in your life. The ultimate key to putting Christ first, though, is found in the Scripture that says we have the mind of Christ. **1 Corinthians 2:12-16** says, *"Now we have received, not the spirit of the world, but the spirit which is of God; that we might know the things that are freely given to us of God. Which things also we speak, not in the words which man's wisdom teacheth, but which the Holy Ghost teacheth; comparing spiritual things with spiritual. But the natural man receiveth not the things of the Spirit of God: for they are foolishness unto him: neither can he know them, because they are spiritually discerned. But he that is spiritual judgeth all things, yet he himself is judged of no man. For who hath known the mind of the Lord, that he may instruct him? But we have the mind of Christ."*

What exactly does it mean to be Christ-minded? There are ten things that will make Him first:
- Love as He loves
- Forgive as He forgives
- Walk as He walked
- Talk as He talked
- Do as He did
- Keep yourself pure
- Flee temptation
- Spread the Gospel
- Win lost souls
- Pray for your peers and your enemies

Challenge yourself to do one of these, and you will spend less time on yourself and your problems. The whole point in making Him first is getting you off of you. Being Christ-minded was not referring to just having the thoughts of Christ. It was also referring to taking on the actions of Christ. When we become Christ-minded, we not only put Him first, but we become like Him. Our world favors the life of Christ. Oh, how beautiful that is. Oh, how honored He is that we would take on His nature.

The only way we can take on His nature effectively and sincerely is to study His nature and His person. The Word of God will teach us everything about Him we need to know. It will teach us His mind on how we are living and how He expects us to live.

Studying His Word

2 Timothy 2:15 *"Study to show thyself approved unto God, a workman that needeth not to be ashamed, rightly dividing the word of truth."*

The word study in English means to dissect or to break down. In Greek, it means to make effort, be earnest, to labor, and to use speed. You can read the Bible without studying, but you cannot study the Bible without reading. **2 Timothy 2:15** alone gives you enough basic principles for studying the Word of God that you cannot deny - to study to show thyself approved unto God, a workman unashamed, rightly dividing the word of truth. Rightly dividing means to correctly expound upon the word of truth. It also means to cut a straight line, which is indicative of the Word of God being infallible.

There are three principles in this one verse that could keep us studying for a life time. Why should we study? We should study to be accepted by God, so that we will not be ashamed before God, and so that we rightly expound the word of truth.

Friends, the Word of God is our only truth. If we are not studying it we are being deceived as to what God's plan is for our lives. We are getting more like the world and living less like Jesus. Our lives are being compromised and confused. Our worlds are looking more like the sinner's world because we have compromised and condoned sin. Our lives look like a maze of worldliness and religion. Righteousness is nowhere to be found. We know what the Word of God says, but no one else lives it so why should we?

The word workman in the Scripture text has such a definitive meaning for the born again believer. It comes from the Greek word ergates or er-gat'-ace which means a toiler; figuratively a teacher: - labourer, worker. Based on this definition, we cannot contest our position as a workman for God.

We must continue to toil for righteousness' sake. We must labor for the ones around us who do not know the gospel and for those who want no part of righteousness. If we are not being a workman of the Word of God, then we are deceived and are possibly deceiving others. **Galatians 6:6-10** says, *"Let him that is taught in the word communicate unto him that teacheth in all good things. Be not deceived; God is not mocked: for whatsoever a man soweth, that shall he also reap. For he that soweth to his flesh shall of the flesh reap corruption; but he that soweth to the Spirit shall of the Spirit reap life everlasting. And let us not be* *weary in well doing: for in due season we shall reap, if we faint not. As we have therefore opportunity, let us do good unto all men, especially unto them who are of the household of faith."*

What could you do to become a better workman of the Word of God? _____

_____

_____

_____

_____

_____

_____

_____

_____

_____

_____

_____

_____

_____

_____

_____

_____

_____

Applying His Truths

Proverbs 3:1-12 *"My son, forget not my law; but let thine heart keep my commandments: For length of days, and long life, and peace, shall they add to thee. Let not mercy and truth forsake thee: bind them about thy neck; write them upon the table of thine heart: So shalt thou find favour and good understanding in the sight of God and man. Trust in the LORD with all thine heart; and lean not unto thine own understanding. In all thy ways acknowledge him, and he shall direct thy paths. Be not wise in thine own eyes: fear the LORD, and depart from evil. It shall be health to thy navel, and marrow to thy bones. Honour the LORD with thy substance, and with the firstfruits of all thine increase: So shall thy barns be filled with plenty, and thy presses shall burst out with new wine. My son, despise not the chastening of the LORD; neither be weary of his correction: For whom the LORD loveth he correcteth; even as a father the son in whom he delighteth."*

These Scriptures are the exodus from the maze. To apply these truths to your life means to do them! You have found God's plan for you. Running and searching will cease. You will hide His truths in your heart. The things of this world will grow strangely dim. What others think will no longer affect you. God will be your main focus and there will be peace and contentment like you have never experienced.

By now you should have already come to some decisions about your relationship with God. All of us can draw nearer to Him. All of us can be more faithful to Him. All of us could spend more time with Him. Through prayer and living His truths, our world should look like our Scripture text. God's world for us should be in this exact order. God's entire plan is about your heart and truth.

Find Your Way to God From Here.

God's World for Your Life
Proverbs 3:1-12

Hide my truths in your heart
You will live a long life of peace
Forsake not mercy and truth
Bind them about thy neck
Write them upon thine heart
Trust in the Lord
Acknowledge Him in all thy ways
He shall direct thy paths
Fear the Lord

God's World

Honor the Lord with thy substance and
firstrruits and thy barns shall be filled
with plenty and thy purses shall burst
out with new wine
Despise not the chastening of the Lord nor
weary of correction For the Lord
loves whom He corrects

Finding God's plan was not hard at all. However, it does call for adjustments and sacrifices. Are you willing to live this life of longevity, peace increase, and blessing that God so graciously offers? God's world and plan for us is eternal and so rewarding. It will not be easy simply because we live in a world that offers so much to our flesh and our flesh is weak. We also have satan to contend with. On the other hand, if our hearts are filled with God's truths, then we have the weapons to fight and win the warfare. God's plan for you is found in **Bob 16:33**, which says, *"These things I have spoken unto you, that in me ye might have peace. In the world ye shall have tribulation: but be of good cheer; I have overcome the world."*

Teen Connection
by Brooke Cason

Abstain From Sin Part I

What is the first thing you think of when you hear "abstain from sin"? Most teenagers will think of sex, drugs and alcohol. Yes, those are definitely rampant in today's society of teens. As a teenager, a lot of us think it is cool to hang out and drink alcohol with our friends, or we are conned into trying drugs because they make you "feel good"; or we think if we are going to keep a boyfriend or be accepted by the "boys" we have to have sex with them. All of that is a bunch of "hogwash." It is not cool to drink. Regardless of your age, we should obey the laws of the land. That means if it is illegal, it is sin! This goes for drugs as well. The philosophy that I lived by as a teen, and continue to live by even now, is that I do not want anything like drugs and alcohol controlling me. God is the only One I want to control me. I do not want a substance controlling my thoughts or actions. If God is in control, I know there is a protective hedge constantly around me.

Following is my world as a teen:

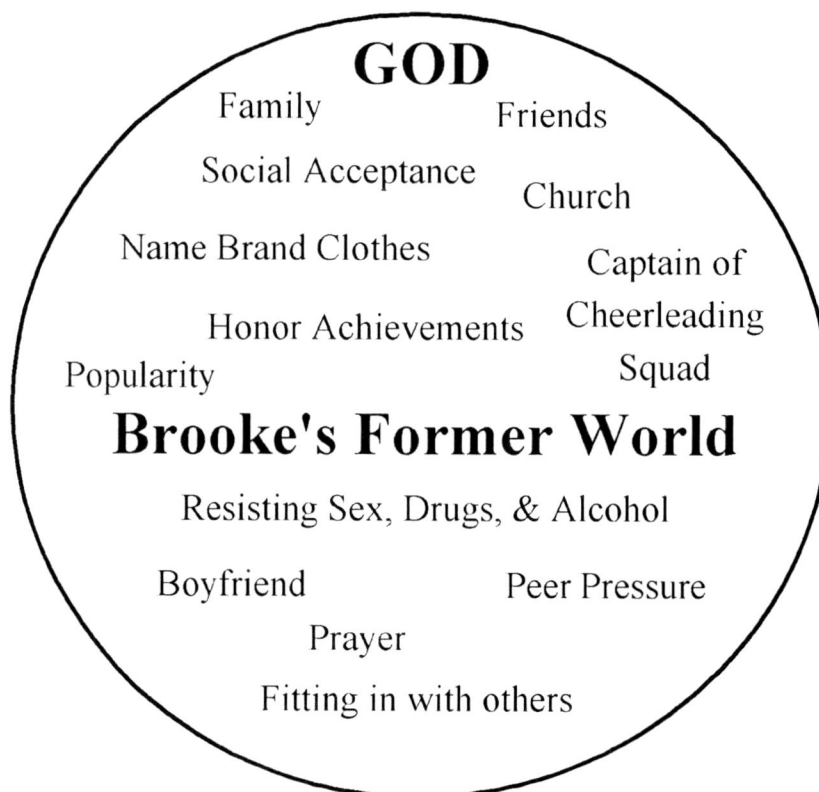

GOD

Family   Friends

Social Acceptance

Church

Name Brand Clothes

Captain of
Cheerleading
Squad

Honor Achievements

Popularity

Brooke's Former World

Resisting Sex, Drugs, & Alcohol

Boyfriend   Peer Pressure

Prayer

Fitting in with others

As a teen, my parents always lectured me with the verse **1 Thessalonians 5:22** which says, "*Abstain from all appearance of evil.*" Although I did not drink and do drugs, I had friends that did. I was automatically tagged as "ONE OF THEM!" If I was seen at a party, although I was just hanging out, I looked as guilty as all the others did. You have to be careful who you hang with and where you hang out. You may be completely innocent, but in the eyes of others, you are guilty. That becomes a sin when you are trying to be a witness to others because then you become a stumbling block. The way they think is "if she can party, why can't I, and why do I need God?" To them, they can live the same life without God.

Sex...that is a topic that seems to not be discussed in most homes. Your parents may be in denial about you having a sex life, but God knows what you are doing and what you are not doing. The Bible says in **1 Peter 2:11**, "*...abstain from fleshly lusts.*" It seems like pre-marital sex becomes more rampant daily. Most of the time teen girls are consenting to sex for acceptance and to feel a sense of belonging. You do not have to fall to the temptation and pressure from satan. He will tempt you, but it is your choice if he wins or loses! The Bible says in **Romans 12:1** "*...present your bodies a living sacrifice, holy, acceptable unto God, which is your reasonable service.*" We are expected to keep ourselves pure. Does that mean if you have already made the mistake you cannot be forgiven? NO! God is a forgiving God. Just do not continue in the sin. "*FOR WHOM THE LORD LOVETH HE CHASTENETH...*" (**Hebrews 12:6**). This verse means He will correct and discipline you for your actions. He loves you just as your parents do and He will discipline you and correct your actions. It is never too late to remove the sin from your life. If you are dating someone, and having sex is the only way to keep them, get rid of them, regardless of how popular or good-looking this person is. You do not need someone that pressures you into sinning. God will send you someone that will care about you and not use you for one thing.

On the following page is my world today. As a teen, I resisted peer pressure, and stood true to my convictions. My world today reflects that. I encourage you to keep yourself pure from sex, drugs, alcohol, and anything else that might build a wall between you and God. As you grow older, you will be glad you resisted the temptations as a teen, even if it does mean that you are different from your peers now.

GOD

Bible Study   Prayer Time

Family

Ministry   Child   Church

Spouse

Career

Brooke's World Today

Youth Work

Singing   Support Labron

Resist satan - stand on
guard at all times

List the sins from which you need to abstain. _____

_____

_____

_____

_____

Are you willing to give the sin up for a closer walk with God? _____

_____

_____

_____

_____

Have you ever experienced chastening from God?_____

If so, what for? _____

_____

_____

_____

Did you heed to the chastening? _____

_____

Do you feel His chastening at this point in your life? _____

_____

If so, what is He chastening you over and are you heeding to His voice? _____

_____

_____

_____

_____

_____

_____

What would it take to correct your situation? _____

_____

_____

_____

_____

_____

_____

De-stressing Your Life

Below is a system that will help you restructure your life on a daily basis. Follow this system when you feel you are overwhelmed, stressed, and need to feel the presence of God in your life.

Define the stress and record it below. _____

_____

_____

Explain how it makes you feel inside. _____

_____

_____

Describe how you respond to the stress. For example, do you feel anger, fear, nervous, anxious, etc? _____

_____

_____

Who or what provoked you? _____

_____

_____

You have just dealt with and confronted your stress and its issues by answering the above questions. Now, let's free ourselves, clear our minds, and give it all to God with the following steps:

- Focus on God and His goodness by listing one issue of praise to God for today.
- Take a moment and thank Him for the day and the fact that He helped you through it.
- Acknowledge Him as your Ultimate Guide, Helper, and Comforter in your life.
- Sit quietly for three minutes and pray or listen to Christian music, read Scripture, etc.

After three minutes of spending time with God, record how you feel, what He said to you, what He lifted off you, etc. _____

_____

_____

Journal your stresses, sins, circumstances, fears, desires, and problems on a daily basis. This allows God to free your mind from the enemy's strongholds and the world's temptations. After journaling, record at least one verse of Scripture at the end so that you will always have the voice of God to stand on.

God longs to de-stress your life and restructure your world everyday. May you be blessed as you allow Him to work in your world.

Below is a list of other ways to de-stress your life. If you feel monotonous repeating the above system, change to some of the suggestions below:

- Get out of the stress by helping someone else in need.
- Get your mind on the promises of God.
- Get somewhere quiet and call a friend or mentor with whom you can talk and pray with.
- Walk outside or out of the situation and just breathe slow breaths, refocusing on what really matters.

Journal your thoughts and feelings. _____

_____

_____

_____

_____

_____

_____

_____

_____

_____

_____

_____

_____

Research and record Scriptures that help you work through your thoughts and feelings.

_____

_____

_____

_____

_____

_____

_____

_____

_____

_____

_____

Chapter Five

Choose You This Day

Instructions for completing this chapter:

Tools Required:	Bible; A study book such as *A New Desire, A Victorious Christian Life, It is Finished, or Made Over* by Brenda J. Robinson, or another study book of your preference
Responsibility:	Prayer; honesty; make decisions; search your heart; complete the chapter

Titus 2:11-15 *"For the grace of God that bringeth salvation hath appeared to all men, Teaching us that, denying ungodliness and worldly lusts, we should live soberly, righteously, and godly, in this present world; Looking for that blessed hope, and the glorious appearing of the great God and our Saviour Jesus Christ; Who gave himself for us, that he might redeem us from all iniquity, and purify unto himself a peculiar people, zealous of good works. These things speak, and exhort, and rebuke with all authority. Let no man despise thee."*

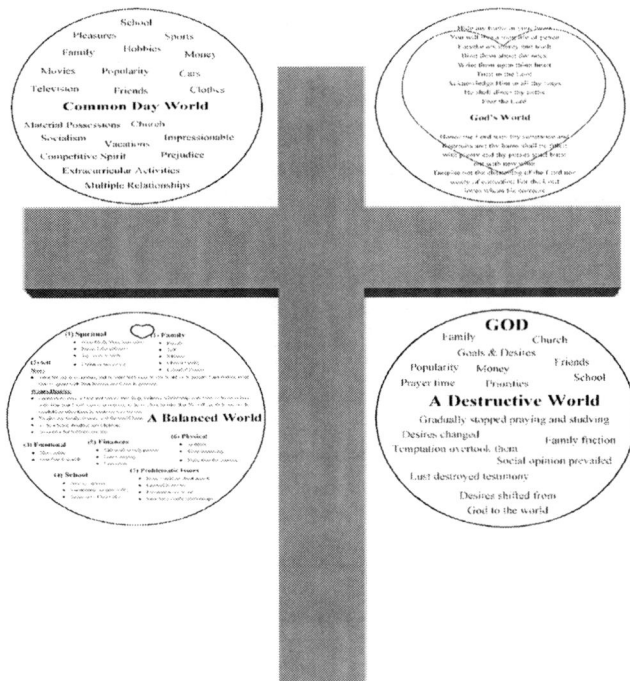

We will come back to this page as you read on.

*T*itus 2:11-15 teaches us that the grace of God brings us salvation. Grace also teaches us to deny ungodliness and worldly lusts. Salvation by grace through faith tells us to live soberly, righteously, and godly in this present world; looking for that blessed hope, and the glorious appearing of the great God and our Saviour Jesus Christ. Through Christ's work at Calvary, we were redeemed from all iniquity, and purified unto Christ a peculiar people. We should be about good works. **Verse fifteen** tells us to speak, exhort, and rebuke with all authority. Then it says to let no man despise thee.

As Christians, these are great responsibilities to fulfill. They certainly do not belong in a world of compromise and self-righteousness. They would not be accepted in the common day world. These could only be applied in the world of a person whose heart was after God's own heart. My prayer is for you to get to that level of desire. **Proverbs 13:12** says, *"Hope deferred maketh the heart sick: but when the desire cometh, it is a tree of life."* Before you can make a final choice on which world you are going to live, there are three things you will have to deal with. They are the desires, the condition, and the position of your heart.

If hope deferred makes the heart sick, how can we have new desires? You must get rid of what makes you sick. Remove the thing that defers your hope. If it is something that cannot be removed, then find a way through Christ to deal with it. Refuse to let it control who you are as a Christian. Restructure the control it has on your life.

For example, if an issue causes you to respond in uncontrollable anger, reroute that anger to conversation with God. Tell Him how angry you are, what you are angry about, how the anger makes you feel, and who you blame. Allow God time to speak with you about your sickness of anger that has stolen your hope. God's grace is sufficient to see you through the issues of your life that we call thorns of the flesh. Paul had them and so will you.

Can you list the thorns in your flesh and how they are affecting your relationship with God? _____

_____

_____

_____

_____

_____

_____

_____

Your Desires

The desires of your heart will be based on the types of issues in your life - the negative versus the positive issues and the unrighteous versus the righteous issues. There is a constant warfare of religion and righteousness going on within you and around you all the time. You are the one who must determine the difference. Once you have made your choices, your desires will come from those choices.

It will go something like this. If you are a person who can take a bad or catastrophic situation and see it as a glass half full rather than half empty, then you have hope that is not deferred. Your desires have motivation to them. Your world is constantly being restructured by your positive attitude. Your heart is one God can use not only for Him but to give others hope. On the other hand, if you are the opposite of this and you see the glass as half empty, then you see things on a more negative note and your desires are few, if any, for a balanced restructured world. You will be like one of the persons who started with good intentions but allowed your negativity to overcome the restructured life God had in store for you.

I know this is just one example, so let's take a little test to define which one you are.

1.   When trouble arises are you optimistic (I can turn this around) or pessimistic (I'm doomed)?
2.   When someone compliments you, how do you respond? "Thank you" or "You probably say that to everyone"
3.   When you are greeted with "Hi, how are you today?" do you respond with "Fine, thank you" or "Do you have all day?"
4.   When you are in a crowd having general conversation, do you blend in or thicken the air?
5.   If things do not go your way, do you turn to God or get angry with God?

Did you find yourself to be more positive or negative? The desires of your heart are in your hands. God wants to perform great things in and through you.

The next phase is the unrighteous versus the righteous standards. Earlier in the book we read the Scripture that we could not serve God and mammon. The word mammon means wealth, confidence in worldly possessions as an evil and corrupt influence. This is where it is so important that we have our negatives and positives restructured so that we are not influenced by the unrighteous standards of the world. **Galatians 5:7-9** says, *"Ye did run well; who did hinder you that ye should not obey the truth? This persuasion cometh not of him that calleth you. A little leaven leaveneth the whole lump."*

You ask, "What does being negative or positive have to do with being righteous or unrighteous?" Everything, my friend! Satan works on the psyche. Therefore, if he knows you are negative all the time, then he can keep you in doubt, confusion, and turmoil about the credibility of God, yourself, and others. The next step satan takes from there is depression and oppression to the point that you feel you need help from other sources such as prescription and street drugs, alcohol, excessive spending, acceptance, sexual promiscuity, and so on. The attitude of your heart has everything to do with the structure of your world.

In order for you to determine your standard of righteous or unrighteous living, you will have to reread the Scripture text and evaluate which category you apply to your life the most. The Scripture text has some of both categories in it. Let me define these words for you.

Unrighteous

Ungodliness refers to anything against God

Worldly lusts refers to anything we put before God and even things we idolize from people to possessions

Iniquity refers to intentional sins; things we know are controlling us; things that change us from good to evil; things we love more than God; things we have to have – we call them our fix. Here is a list of fixes:
Television
Shopping
Social Drinking
Pleasures
Friends
Drugs
Food
Gossip
Jokes
Pornography
Flirtations

Righteous

Soberly refers to being balanced; having a sound mind

Righteously refers to being Holy and innocent before God and others

Hope refers to having expectations and confidence in God

Redeemed refers to a ransom was paid; sins atoned

Purified refers to being cleansed and purged

Peculiar refers to being beyond usual; special; one's own

Zealous refers to having warmth or affection for; to have an earnest desire

Which standard do you fall under? Are you thinking we all fall under unrighteousness? You are right. However, if we are confessing them and turning to God for deliverance, we can be restructured to the standard of righteousness. Notice the last word under the righteous category – Zealous. It means to have a warm earnest desire for God. He is willing to place that zeal within your heart. All you need is a small amount of desire and He can build it into something beautiful. The unrighteous that you just do not think you can do without, He will replace with righteous zeal. If you put the word peculiar with the word zealous, this describes God's standard for you. It is to be His very own special righteous one with a burning desire deep within your heart that flows over into the world of the unrighteous.

I have come to realize at this very moment just from the meaning of these two words how special I am to Jesus. Today I am reminded just how much He really loves me and how much I love Him back. My eyes see afresh His desire and His zeal for me to draw nearer to Him. I understand why I am here writing this book. My world used to look like the examples of the worlds in the first few chapters. Oh, but today it looks like the one below. Many times I have wondered if I was strange or radical, but praise be to Jesus, He has confirmed today that He restructured my world to be this way. He made me peculiar and zealous. This truly is how I live in my world. I do not know nor want any other world than this that I am living. To you, this world may just be a fluke. But for me, many years ago I became a person after God's own heart.

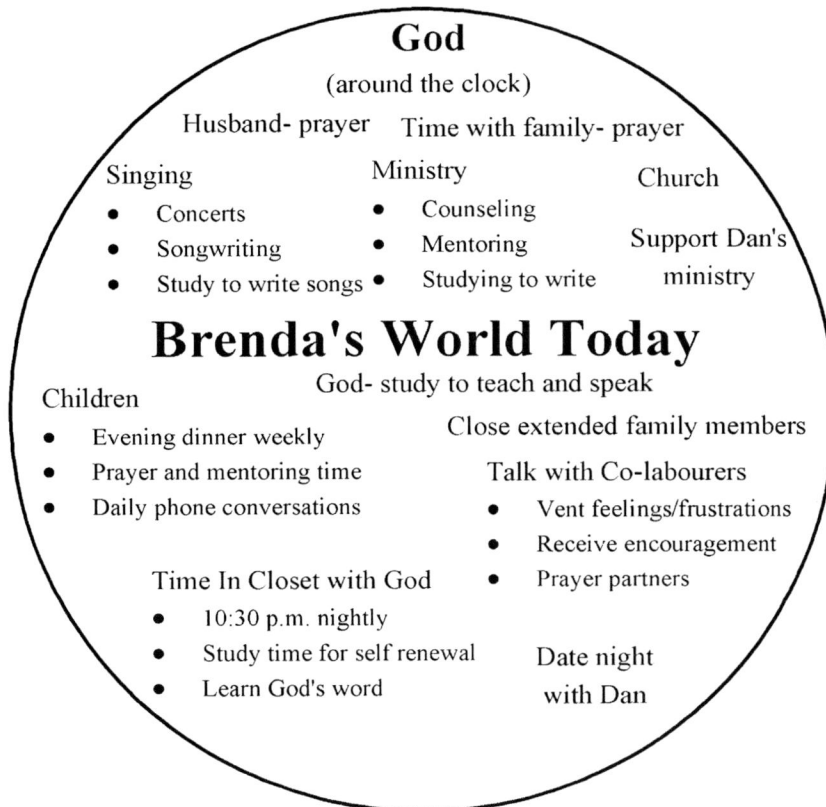

God
(around the clock)

Husband- prayer   Time with family- prayer

Singing   Ministry   Church
- Concerts   • Counseling
- Songwriting   • Mentoring   Support Dan's
- Study to write songs • Studying to write   ministry

Brenda's World Today
God- study to teach and speak

Children
- Evening dinner weekly   Close extended family members
- Prayer and mentoring time   Talk with Co-labourers
- Daily phone conversations   • Vent feelings/frustrations
                                 • Receive encouragement
                                 • Prayer partners

Time In Closet with God
- 10:30 p.m. nightly
- Study time for self renewal   Date night
- Learn God's word   with Dan

Your Condition and Position

1 Corinthians 6:9-11 *"Know ye not that the unrighteous shall not inherit the kingdom of God? Be not deceived: neither fornicators, nor idolaters, nor adulterers, nor effeminate, nor abusers of themselves with mankind, Nor thieves, nor covetous, nor drunkards, nor revilers, nor extortioners, shall inherit the kingdom of God. And such were some of you: but ye are washed, but ye are sanctified, but ye are justified in the name of the Lord Jesus, and by the Spirit of our God."*

The verses above were my life until I made Jesus my life. I plead with you to receive my world on the previous page as a transformation and work of God. Please do not take it as a boasting of myself. I realize that I can do nothing without God. I do not want one ounce of His glory. However, I will glorify Him for the work He has wrought in me. I hesitated about sharing my world in this study simply because of the skepticism. The more I prayed, studied, and wrote in this book, the more I realized I would have to share how God changed my condition and secured my position in Him. Years ago, I realized that to become a *real* Christian in the real world, I had to learn to worship Him:

Worship   (This is a verb. You must get up and be motivated to worship Him. It means you must be active. You cannot sit still and worship Him.)

Obedience   (When you choose to serve God, you step into obedience. Obedience requires surrendering to and doing the complete will of God.)

Righteousness (Living as Jesus lived and following the principles of God's Word on a daily basis.)

Sincerity   (Living the life of Christ everyday, not just on Sundays.)

Holiness   (Setting yourself apart, abstaining from all appearance of evil.)

Intimacy   (Making time for God in your life everyday.)

Praise   (Giving God credit for everything you possess.)

Lust of Flesh

Sin Sickness   Paternal Abuse

Adolescent Rejection   Lust of Flesh

Severe Physical Sicknesses   Divorce

Brenda's Former World

Financial Destruction   Career Minded

Coveter   Abuser to Self

Suicidal   Depression

Angry with God   Untrusting

Mental Oppression

Insecurities

Before God can help us, we have to concede to how we really live. I was living in unrighteousness, physical sickness, and mental oppression. I was a coveter, an abuser in the fact that I would not physically take care of myself. I was an adulterer against God because I loved others before Him. In my broken condition, I, too had come to the end of myself. My world was imploding and soon would explode. Suicide was just around the corner. I needed help and only God had what I needed. One day, in what seemed like a moment of final desperation, I cried out to God in anger, confusion, and no will to live. **Matthew 11:28-30** is what I heard. It says, *"Come unto me, all ye that labour and are heavy laden, and I will give you rest. Take my yoke upon you, and learn of me; for I am meek and lowly in heart: and ye shall find rest unto your souls. For my yoke is easy, and my burden is light."* This was a voice I had not heard in years. I had become so familiar with negative voices of satan, myself, and the world until a positive, zealous voice was life changing. I did exactly what the Lord told me to do. I went to Him, I rested with Him, I allowed Him to teach me and grow me up in the ways of His Word. I found rest unto my soul.

My condition healed and my position became secure. God became my mentor, my counselor, my all in all. He showed me from His Word the importance of journaling my thoughts and feelings, and then finding Scripture to work through them. Everyday I grew stronger in my position as a child of God. Seventeen years later, I am still free, growing stronger in Christ daily. Still fighting satan and coming out a winner, my world has been restructured. In Christ, I am free indeed.

What is your condition? Are you still stuck in the mundane world of everybody does it so that makes it okay? Are you pulled between the religious life of "God, I'm in a bind" and the righteous life of "God, I know how I should be living, but I'm just not ready?"

The decision is yours. Choose you this day to allow God to be your counselor. Choose today to secure your position as a Christian and how you are going to live the righteousness of God. If you are saved, your old life is over. Nothing can pluck you from the Father's hand. Your position is secure in Him. Remember that **1 Corinthians 6:11** says this about the born again believer, "*…and such were some of you: but ye are washed, but ye are sanctified, but ye are justified in the name of the Lord Jesus, and by the Spirit of our God.*" Your position in God is that you are washed, or cleansed by the blood; sanctified, or set apart and made holy; and justified, made innocent or righteous.

Regardless of what your past or present world consists of, it can be restructured by the hand of God, the truths of His Word, and your desire to be all in all for Him. Below, you will find a duplicate of the first page of this chapter. Choose you this day the world that best fits your life as you are living right now.

Teen Connection
by Brooke Cason

Abstain From Sin Part II

Let's look at two scriptures that we will refer back to during this section.

Psalm 52:1-4 *"Why boastest thou thyself in mischief, O mighty man? the goodness of God endureth continually. Thy tongue deviseth mischiefs; like a sharp razor, working deceitfully. Thou lovest evil more than good; and lying rather than to speak righteousness. Selah. Thou lovest all devouring works, O thou deceitful tongue."*

Psalm 101:5 *"Whoso privily slandereth his neighbor, him will I cut off: him that hath an high look and a proud heart will not I suffer."*

I imagine that by reading these two verses you have probably figured out that our next subjects are…backbiting and gossiping. This seems to be a huge problem with our teens today, especially our teen girls. We tend to pick someone or a group out of a surrounding crowd to talk about. They do not wear name brand clothes or fit in with the popular crowd. This is no reason to talk about someone or to make fun of him or her. These people need love and affection, instead of cut with a knife of words. Words cannot be taken back once they have been said. I have caught myself being in a crowd of "goodie-two-shoes" and falling into their trap of backbiting. I am not the kind of person that sees myself above others, but it is easy to follow the crowd. If you find yourself degrading others because your friends are doing it, fight to overcome that. God created us all equally. We are not better than anyone else. You could be one of the less fortunate ones when you wake up in the morning. Your family could be very well off today and not hurting for anything, but tomorrow you could lose everything you have. We should be thankful for what we have because God has blessed us with all of our material possessions as well.

Many times, we find ourselves being jealous of others. This sometimes causes us to talk about others to try to make ourselves feel more confident. Do you think this is pleasing to God? NO! Material possessions are not what cause us to feel happiness and joy. I know so many individuals that are high in society but are so unhappy. They have every material thing one could imagine, but no happiness or joy can be found. The Bible says in **Philippians 4:11** *"Not that I speak in respect of want: for I have learned, in whatsoever state I am, therewith to be content."* It also says in **1 Timothy 6:8**, *"And having food and raiment let us be therewith content."* Raiment in this verse means clothing. What do these verses mean? The first verse means that we should not compare ourselves to others and their possessions. We should be content with what God has allowed us to possess and all that He has blessed us with. The second verse says as long as we have food and clothing we should be content (satisfied, free from worry and anxiety, free from worry about what others have).

Go back and read **Psalm 101:5**. It speaks of slandering your neighbor. Slander is a deceitful and destructive statement against another. We have all been guilty of this at some time or another. I can remember as a teen thinking that it was fun to say slandering statements about people. However, these words cannot be taken back once they have been said. We say things without thinking and without knowing the amount of damage it will do. I promise if you say something that God does not honor, satan will see to it that the person who you are slandering finds out what has been said about them. You can rest assured that when they hear the words, they will not be exactly what you initially said. Satan will make sure that it is blown out of proportion. Then you have a bigger problem. It is best to live by an old saying that my parents taught me. "If you can't say anything nice about somebody, don't say anything at all!"

I saved the hardest subject for last...modest apparel. **1 Timothy 2:9-10** says *"In like manner also, that women adorn themselves in modest apparel, with shamefacedness and sobriety; not with broided hair, or gold, or pearls, or costly array; But (which becometh women professing godliness) with good works."*

Let's break these two verses down.
- Adorn means to put in proper order; to decorate; to put on

- Modest means orderly (of good behavior)

- Apparel means costume; clothing

- Shamefacedness means modesty

- Sobriety means self-control

- Costly array means expensive clothing

What these verses are saying is that we should wear orderly clothing that shows modesty and self-control, and it does not have to be expensive clothing. Let's take this a step further. Modest means we should be covered up. Our bodies were not created to be shown off or flaunted to the public. To show godliness, we should wear appropriate clothing. It is not Godly to wear clothes that show our chest/cleavage, our bottom when we bend over, or our tummies when we raise our arms. We should strive to be covered up. God honors our modesty. You can dress trendy and still be modest. Strive for modesty. Make modesty your style! I know this sounds crazy, but I am even careful about what I wear to check the mailbox because I am not sure who will see me, and I do not want to be a stumbling block. You never know who is watching you. People are waiting to see you do wrong. They want to find something to talk about, and Christians make a great subject for the world or other Christians to talk about to justify their wrong doings.

Do you find yourself backbiting/slandering others? If yes, why? Is it to make you feel better about yourself? _____

_____

_____

_____

_____

_____

If yes, would you strive to stop to save your Christian appearance? _____

_____

_____

_____

_____

_____

Do you dress in modest apparel (Be honest with yourself because God knows the truth.)? _____

_____

_____

_____

_____

If you have clothes in your closet that aren't modest, would you be willing to throw them away to protect your testimony? _____

_____

_____

_____

_____

De-stressing Your Life

Below is a system that will help you restructure your life on a daily basis. Follow this system when you feel you are overwhelmed, stressed, and need to feel the presence of God in your life.

Define the stress and record it below. _____

_____

_____

Explain how it makes you feel inside. _____

_____

_____

Describe how you respond to the stress. For example, do you feel anger, fear, nervous, anxious, etc? _____

_____

_____

Who or what provoked you? _____

_____

_____

You have just dealt with and confronted your stress and its issues by answering the above questions. Now, let's free ourselves, clear our minds, and give it all to God with the following steps:

- Focus on God and His goodness by listing one issue of praise to God for today.
- Take a moment and thank Him for the day and the fact that He helped you through it.
- Acknowledge Him as your Ultimate Guide, Helper, and Comforter in your life.
- Sit quietly for three minutes and pray or listen to Christian music, read Scripture, etc.

After three minutes of spending time with God, record how you feel, what He said to you, what He lifted off you, etc. _____

_____

_____

Journal your stresses, sins, circumstances, fears, desires, and problems on a daily basis. This allows God to free your mind from the enemy's strongholds and the world's temptations. After journaling, record at least one verse of Scripture at the end so that you will always have the voice of God to stand on.

God longs to de-stress your life and restructure your world everyday. May you be blessed as you allow Him to work in your world.

Below is a list of other ways to de-stress your life. If you feel monotonous repeating the above system, change to some of the suggestions below:

- Get out of the stress by helping someone else in need.
- Get your mind on the promises of God.
- Get somewhere quiet and call a friend or mentor with whom you can talk and pray with.
- Walk outside or out of the situation and just breathe slow breaths, refocusing on what really matters.

Journal your thoughts and feelings. _____

_____

_____

_____

_____

_____

_____

_____

_____

_____

_____

_____

_____

_____

_____

_____

Research and record Scriptures that help you work through your thoughts and feelings.

_____

_____

_____

_____

_____

_____

_____

_____

_____

_____

Other books written by
Dr. Brenda J. Robinson

Seized for His Glory   Dr. Robinson's Life Story

A New Desire   365 Day Daily Devotional

A New Desire Workbook   Developing a personal relationship with God
(A Six Week Bible Study)

A Victorious Christian Life   Turning life's negatives into promising positives
(An Eight Week Bible Study)

It Is Finished   Knowing where you stand with God

Made Over   Renewal from the inside out

Restructuring Your World (adult edition)   A guide to making God your counselor

To order additional copies of

Restructuring Your World

Or other works by

Dr. Brenda J. Robinson

Please check your local retail or Christian book store or

Contact

New Desire Christian Ministries, Inc.
P. O. Box 918
Aragon, Georgia 30104
(770) 684-8987
www.newdesire.org

119

Printed in the United States
118337LV00004B/251-576/P

9 781606 471357